I am Joseph

(It Couldn't Happen to a Nicer Guy)

ALAN PAIN

Illustrated by Sue Lea

KINGSWAY PUBLICATIONS
EASTBOURNE

First published 1990
Reprinted 1991

Front cover illustration by Taffy Davies

British Library Cataloguing in Publication Data

Pain, Alan
I am Joseph.
I. Title
823'.914 [F]
ISBN 0-86065-725-6

Printed in Great Britain for
KINGSWAY PUBLICATIONS LTD
1 St Anne's Road, Eastbourne, E. Sussex BN21 3UN by
BPCC Hazell Books, Aylesbury, Bucks.
Member of BPCC Ltd.
Typeset by Nuprint Ltd, Harpenden, Herts

To our three children
who make parenthood a good laugh.

To Rebecca,
for constant interruptions and incessant questions.

To Elizabeth,
for a strict diet of crackerbread, celery
and thick chocolate cake.

To Andrew,
for supporting Arsenal in Villa country,
even when we lose.

Contents

Introduction

Like most Sunday-school children, I grew up knowing Joseph, but almost exclusively as a spoiled young man who had pretentious dreams and a flamboyant coat. After all, you can't expect five-year-olds to understand why Joseph refused to be a toy-boy for Potiphar's wife! Better to keep the youngster in blissful ignorance until he can cope with the sordid games of adult life.

More recently, two music-student daughters and one potential music-student son have battered me night and day with their varied renderings of *Joseph and His Amazing Technicolour Dreamcoat*, and that has reminded me how much more there is to Joseph than the early offerings of Sunday school (or have you changed the name to Family Church?). If the secular world finds successful entertainment in Joseph, we can expect to find material which makes for relevant and arresting teaching.

The story of Joseph, which scholars like to call 'the Joseph saga', occupies more than a quarter of the Book of Genesis—chapters 37–50—in a penetrating study of human relationships, especially those of family life: marriage, fatherhood, motherhood and childhood. They form the background to the domestic and social upheavals which pursued Joseph from his own land into Egypt, but they are also woven into the overriding theme of the means God uses to guide a man from public disgrace to national acclaim—despite the setbacks of assault, betrayal and prison—bringing him at last to the destiny promised him in his teenage dreams.

We must resist the temptation to hurry into a New Testament application of Joseph. His adventures stand in their own right as a way of teaching us how to cope with family life today. We live in a society which often sneers at Christian values, but produces some appalling casualties for lack of them.

The idea for an imaginary autobiography of Joseph came from a similar treatment of Jeremiah which made me wonder if other biblical characters might enjoy speaking for themselves. A healthy family still offers unique security and a lot of laughs. Joseph illustrates the tragedy of its breakdown and the wonder of its repair, and that calls for our attention.

But let Joseph speak for himself, he's itching to get stuck into the full story, and we shouldn't hold him back any longer.

I

A Chequered Background

If truth is stranger than fiction, my story is the one you must read. It combines family intrigue, deceitful ancestry, malicious hatred, murderous jealousy, sexual drama, incredible rescue, prophetic dreams, sudden twists of fortune, drastic famine, meteoric rise to political power and final reconciliation in an intricate plot which no novelist could have created. I am Joseph, son of Jacob and Rachel.

I am an old man now, without much time left, but the benefits of hindsight reveal the amazing guidance of God. His will has been much more than an individual's whim for my protection and promotion. I can't see far ahead, but a spiritual instinct which is deeper than a gut feeling assures me that I am one of the Patriarchs who prepare the way to an eventful future for our people. Our national fortunes will change and a greater leader than me will arise to forge the rescue of a shattered people. I do not fully understand why we find ourselves in Egypt now, but of this I am sure—there will be high drama when we leave.

My family background is riddled with deception, giving me a chequered moral history. This has caused me to battle for years with a persistent tendency to intrigue which I like to believe did not originate with me but was inherited.

My great grandfather was Abraham. He went to Egypt because of a serious famine in his own country (Gen 12:10). The Egyptians may not exactly shine in our subsequent history, but we have been quick enough to turn to them for help when we have been desperate for food. At the moment we're not in constant conflict with them, and there is no reason to imagine that we will be in the future, but I can't say I feel optimistic about it. There, in Egypt, Abraham feared for his own life, especially if it became known that Sarah was his wife. To save his own skin, he passed her off as his sister, fully aware that the husband of such a beautiful woman was in far greater danger in an alien land than her brother. Pharaoh was horrified when he discovered the truth. 'What have you done to me?...Why didn't you tell me she was your wife? Why did you say, "She is my sister," so that I took her to be my wife? Now then, here is your wife. Take her and go' (Gen 12:18–19). The story has passed into our folk-history, always to be told with wicked amusement and a total absence of remorse.

Isaac, my paternal grandfather, learned quickly from his father's example. He faced a further famine in which he became convinced that God did not want him to travel to Egypt. He went instead to the country of the Philistines, where Abimelech was king (Gen 26:1). There Isaac repeated the deceit practised by his father, pretending that Rebekah was his sister rather than his wife. 'When the men of that place asked him about his wife, he said, "She is my sister," because he was afraid to say, "She is my wife." He thought, "The men of this place might kill me on account of Rebekah, because she is beautiful" ' (Gen 26:7). Brave men were my ancestors! Isaac grew careless as well as impatient in his deceit, and was spotted one day caressing Rebekah in a way that no man caresses his sister. Abimelech did not need to be shrewd to realise he'd

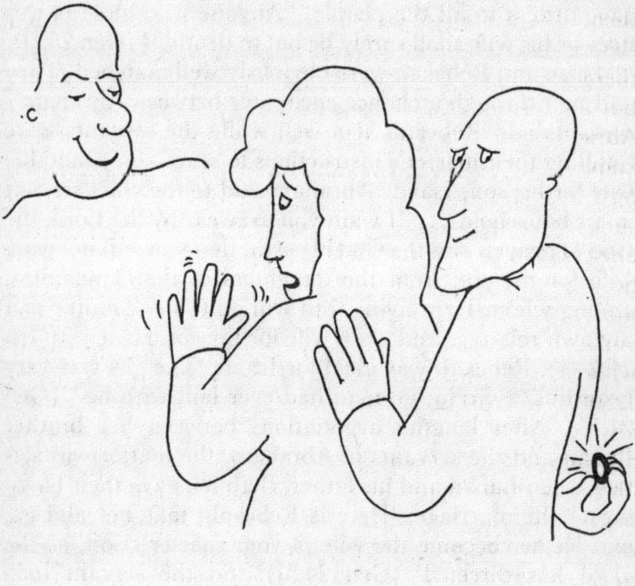

been sold a lie. 'So Abimelech summoned Isaac and said, "She is really your wife! Why did you say, 'She is my sister?' " ' (Gen 26:9). Isaac was one of those men who always seem to land on their feet, and his unmasked deception which might well have cost another man his life won him protection rather than downfall. 'Abimelech gave orders to all the people, "Anyone who molests this man or his wife shall surely be put to death" ' (Gen 26:11).

Isaac and Rebekah were obviously well matched. They had met through a chance encounter between Abraham's servants and Rebekah at a well while the servants were fulfilling their master's instructions to search for a suitable wife for his son, Isaac. 'Abraham said to the chief servant in his household..., "I want you to swear by the Lord, the God of heaven and the God of earth, that you will not get a wife for my son from the daughters of the Canaanites, among whom I am living, but will go to my country and my own relatives and get a wife for my son Isaac" ' (Gen 24:2–4). Rebekah was ideal for Isaac; 'The girl was very beautiful, a virgin; no man had ever lain with her' (Gen 24:16). After lengthy negotiations between her brother Laban and the servants of Abraham, the matter was settled when Laban and his father, Bethuel, gave their blessing to the marriage: 'Here is Rebekah; take her and go, and let her become the wife of your master's son, as the Lord has directed' (Gen 24:51). 'So the servant took Rebekah and left' (Gen 24:61). 'Isaac brought her into the tent of his mother, Sarah, and he married Rebekah' (Gen 24:67).

Rebekah was cunning as well as beautiful and she happily traded on Isaac's doting love for her. She knew he had inherited the considerable wealth of his father, Abraham, and she schemed tirelessly for the advantage of my father, Jacob (Gen 25:5). He was the younger of twin boys born to Isaac and Rebekah, and was clearly the apple of his mother's eye, while the stronger, elder brother, Esau, was his father's favourite. 'The boys grew up, and Esau became a skilful hunter, a man of the open country, while Jacob was a quiet man, staying among the tents. Isaac, who had a taste for wild game, loved Esau, but Rebekah loved Jacob' (Gen 25:27–28).

My father quickly absorbed the example set by his parents. As children copy those around them, so Jacob followed the lead given by Isaac and Rebekah. He held his hungry brother to ransom, and screwed his birthright from him. 'Once when Jacob was cooking some stew, Esau came in from the open country, famished. He said to Jacob, "Quick, let me have some of that red stew! I'm famished!"...Jacob replied, "First sell me your birthright" ' (Gen 25:29–31). 'So he swore an oath to him, selling his birthright to Jacob. Then Jacob gave Esau some bread and some lentil stew.... So Esau despised his birthright' (Gen 25:33–34). As far as I'm concerned, the offer of lentil stew would be nearer blackmail than bribery, a deterrent rather than an incentive, but each man to his own poison. Esau gulped down lentil stew and 'despised his birthright'.

My grandmother, Rebekah, had been biding her time for the final bid to establish her favourite son, Jacob, at the expense of Esau. When her opportunity came, she did not waste it. She had watched Esau and his father like a hawk once she sensed Isaac's days were numbered, and nothing was allowed to stand in the way of her malicious plan. She was determined to rob Esau of the father's blessing usually reserved for the firstborn son in order that it might be transferred to my father and her favourite, Jacob.

Rebekah was careful to miss nothing which passed between her husband and her older son. She eavesdropped on every conversation, and one day she overheard Isaac dispatch Esau for a hunting trip. 'Go out to the open country to hunt some wild game for me' (Gen 27:3). Isaac was by now too old and too short-sighted to share in the escapade. As soon as Esau went out, Rebekah acted. She summoned Jacob, ordered the sacrifice of a couple of kid goats, and had them cooked exactly to Isaac's liking, as only a dutiful wife can. Then she took Esau's clothes and dressed Jacob in them, treating him all the time more like a boy than a man. She used the goat-skins to cover his hands and neck in the hope of giving him the likeness of his hairy brother, and she sent him in to his father to play the part of Esau returning from his hunting expedition. Isaac was old, but he wasn't senile, and his suspicions were aroused. How had Esau returned so soon? Didn't it sound like Jacob? Could this really be Esau? The old man was wary as he peered through his failing eyes. Finally, the smell of Esau's clothes convinced him, and the net closed around him. 'When Isaac caught the smell of his clothes, he blessed him and said, "...May God give you of heaven's dew and of earth's richness—an abundance of corn and new wine. May nations serve you and peoples bow down to you. Be lord over your brothers, and may the sons of your mother bow down to you. May those who curse you be cursed and those who bless you be blessed" ' (Gen 27:27–29).

Esau was furious when he realised how the joint conspiracy of his mother and his brother had cheated him out of his father's blessing. Rebekah had no fears for herself but she was wise enough to plan Jacob's immediate escape. 'Your brother Esau is consoling himself with the thought of killing you...Flee at once to my brother Laban in Haran' (Gen 27:42–43). Even then, Rebekah was still scheming. She assured Isaac that this was a marriage expedition for Jacob, and that was enough to secure her husband's blessing for Jacob's journey. 'Take a wife for yourself there, from among the daughters of Laban, your mother's brother. May God Almighty bless you and make you fruitful and increase your numbers until you become a community of peoples' (Gen 28:2–3). It should not surprise you that Jacob's route led him to a well, a beautiful girl, and a flock of sheep, but this time the deception was practised on him and poor old Dad was served with a dose of his own medicine. He fell in love with a young woman called Rachel, my mother. She was keen enough to marry him, but she had an unmarried older sister at home, Leah. Rachel's father, Laban, knew how serious it would be for any girl if a younger sister preceded her in marriage. By some undisclosed trick, probably connected with strong drink, he substituted Leah for Rachel to spend the night with Jacob. My dad did not lack a sense of humour, but the enjoyment of this joke completely eluded him. 'When morning came, there was Leah! So Jacob said to Laban, "What is this you have done to me? I served you for Rachel, didn't I? Why have you deceived me?" ' (Gen 29:25). If only Esau could have heard his brother of all people complain of being the victim of deception! Laban's reply to Jacob was straight to the point: 'It is not our custom here to give the younger daughter in marriage before the older one' (Gen 29:26). A seven-year labour of love was imposed on a man who must have burned with impatience, but Jacob's wait for Rachel proved to be retribution for someone with a family history of deception that ran back to his grandfather.

It's difficult to believe that Leah really benefited from her father's support because Jacob added Rachel to her older sister. It was no secret that he loved Rachel and tolerated her sister, but the security of a husband evidently meant more to Leah than his love. My own feeling is that the result of that preference was calamitous for the relationship between the men who were born to Jacob's women and found themselves thrown together as brothers and half-brothers, caught in a web of jealousy and spite.

The matter was further complicated because of the ease with which Leah conceived children and the difficulty Rachel had in overcoming her own infertility. The physical problem could have been Jacob's, but he had already fathered children by other women, and Rachel was therefore crushed by a bitter sense of failure. It was inevitable that she would vent her feelings on Leah, and she did.

'When Rachel saw that she was not bearing Jacob any children, she became jealous of her sister. So she said to Jacob, "Give me children or I'll die" ' (Gen 30:1). You'll know that that can be easier said than done. As Sarah before her had offered her own servant, Hagar, to Abraham in the desperation of childlessness, so Rachel offered Bilhah to Jacob to ease her own barren predicament, and Bilhah added to the list of mothers who were contributing sons into our family circle. (Gen 16:1–4; 30:3–5). How different my life would have been if my father had restricted himself to one woman, but that thought has not yet been welcomed into our culture. You can't live with wistful regrets whose sole theme is 'if only', and it did come right for Rachel in the end. Finally, wonderfully, she conceived her first child, and I was born. 'Then God remembered Rachel; he listened to her and opened her womb. She became pregnant and gave birth to a son and said, "God has taken away my disgrace." She named him Joseph, and said, "May the Lord add to me another son" ' (Gen 30:22–24).

Jacob, my father, was by now so steeped in trickery that he did not know how to stop himself. The deception he had seen work to apparent advantage in his father, his mother and his grandfather had become a way of life for him. He entered into an agreement with Laban: he, Jacob, would continue to shepherd the flock of Laban as Laban desperately wanted, if he could have every speckled or spotted sheep, lamb and goat (Gen 30:32–34). Crafty he may have been, but my dad knew his sheep and Laban knew a good man when he found one. The two men made their agreement and Jacob went ahead with a strange plot to ensure that healthy livestock went his way and only the weak animals remained for Laban. 'In this way the man [Jacob] grew exceedingly prosperous and came to own large flocks, maidservants and men servants, and camels and donkeys' (Gen 30:42–43). Laban's sons watched my father's progress with growing suspicion and began to murmur menacingly among themselves. Laban too had niggling doubts, and Jacob took due note of a marked change in his uncle's attitude. 'And Jacob noticed that Laban's attitude towards him was not what it had been' (Gen 31:2).

My father was never one to miss the warning signs, and he realised it was high time he left the area. He explained the whole situation to Leah and Rachel who were indignant in their loyalty to him. 'Surely all the wealth that God took away from our father belongs to us and our children. So do whatever God has told you' (Gen 31:16). That's an ideal doctrine of God for prosperity but it's a bit hard when things go wrong. By a remarkable escape from detection, Rachel avoided red-handed exposure in her theft of household idols from her father, and Laban found nothing when he chased and searched her. The entire matter was amicably settled in a strange covenant ceremony between Laban and my father which centred on a pile of stones. 'So Jacob took a stone and set it up as a pillar. He said to his relatives, "Gather some stones."...Laban said, "This heap is a witness between you and me today" ' (Gen 31:45–46, 48). Peace was re-established between the two men, and Laban returned home, sadder but wiser from his encounter with a new son-in-law. 'Early the next morning Laban kissed his grandchildren and his daughters and blessed them. Then he left and returned home' (Gen 31:55). We have no record of his farewell to Jacob.

My confidence in the power of God to guide me, protect me and bring me into the place he has chosen for me is unshakable, and I can see from that how he acts to guard the lives of many others besides me. I marvel at the way my father seemed to emerge unscathed from every scrape in which he landed himself. He lived a charmed life. I don't pretend to understand how it all works, and it will take time and effort to come to a convincing grasp of God's character and his demands upon us. Each new generation will need to ask its own questions, but it will do well to draw on the experience of its predecessors.

Having seen off Laban, my father ran headlong into Esau. In any physical fight, Esau would have won every time, but it always seemed to be Jacob who gained the upper hand. On this occasion, Dad was expecting trouble from a bitter brother who was usually quite prone to be violent. He put Rachel and me at the rear of his entourage to keep us as far from danger as possible, but a very different Esau from the one he expected greeted him. I'm sure that Jacob would never have offered his brother the mercy and love which he received from Esau. How my uncle overcame his bitterness I'll never know, but he completely disarmed a wary Jacob. 'But Esau ran to meet Jacob and embraced him; he threw his arms around his neck and kissed him. And they wept (Gen 33:4). Esau wanted to prolong this new relationship with an offer of an escort for us, but, for once, my father had no desire to push his luck, and he wanted to be away as quickly as possible. 'Then Esau said, "Let us be on our way; I'll accompany you." But Jacob said to him, "...Let my lord go on ahead of his servant, while I move along slowly at the pace of the droves before me and that of the children...." Esau said, "Then let me leave some of my men with you." "But why do that?" Jacob asked.... So that day Esau started on his way back to Seir. Jacob, however, went to Succoth, where he built a place for himself and made shelters for his livestock' (Gen 33:12–17).

None of us was prepared for the death of my mother, Rachel. She was so excited to find herself pregnant again, and I know Dad was thrilled, despite having as many sons as any sane man could want. Childbirth always has an element of risk, and we live in times when it can be positively dangerous. Soon after Mum went into labour, it was obvious that she was in trouble. I don't know how much of these things a young boy was supposed to know, but I listened carefully to adult conversation, as all wise children do, and I heard enough to realise it was serious. There was likely to be bad news as well as good news. The midwife did her best, encouraging my mother all she could, not least with the wonderful news, 'You have another son.' But it was too late. Rachel, who was by now seriously ill, managed no more than the gasp of her baby's name before she died. 'As she breathed her last, for she was dying, she named her son Ben-Oni. But his father named him Benjamin. So Rachel died' (Gen 35:17–19). A pillar marks the spot where my mother was buried, but my father was never the same man again. Several women had borne his children, but there was only one Rachel in his life.

I, Joseph, had eleven brothers, but only Benjamin and I were sons of Jacob and Rachel, the woman of his fondest love. We were bound to be special in his eyes, and he handled his favour with a blatant partiality I enjoyed in boyhood but lived to regret. It changed the course of my life when it combined with my own presumptuous stupidity to provoke my brothers' revenge. They too had been influenced by the deception which flooded our family history, becoming skilled practitioners of the art at my expense. This deceit has acted like a curse on our family, and I have tried hard to break its destructive power. My struggle to live in complete integrity has been a genuine effort to break out into a new future for those who follow us. Only you can judge my success as you read on.

2

Does God Speak?

If you are searching to know God, sooner or later you're bound to ask the question, 'Does God want to speak to us, and does he have the capacity to do so even if he has the will?' You'll want the personal assurance 'God spoke to me.' It's all very well to claim that God has spoken to us, and that's certainly what I'm claiming for myself, but we do need agreed standards by which we assess claims that God has spoken, whether in approval or in judgement. The question tantalises us now and it will continue to tease us. Clearly, it is an intellectual challenge, but it's much more than that. Spiritually, it is urgent. If you're a sceptic, you will probably dismiss all possibility of God communicating with us. May I be so bold as to say that you're suffering from a closed mind on the subject and that you're rather scared of a personal religious experience. But you're also wistful in your deafness to the voice of God. You may feel that it's an arrogant presumption to believe God has spoken, one that is motivated more by wishful thinking than by spiritual integrity. But if you are genuinely enquiring you'll be looking for clues. You will question those who offer personal testimonies, without the need to hide your own interest in the outcome. You will not be embarrassed by a secret hope that a direct word from God will enhance the meaning of your own life.

You may mischievously ask why more women than men seem to believe God has spoken to them. They could be more impressionable, but they could also be more open to God, and that's a rebuke to all men who often imprison themselves in their own masculine prejudice. If you are a believer you will share your experience, not with pride but with the humility of committed faith. You will recognise the temptation to believe that God speaks to those who are particularly worthy of his attention. Of course, you dismiss the temptation, but it doesn't always go away. Ideally, you belong to a community which has learned to sift itself, scrutinising each claim that God has spoken, and comparing it with the truths which are already fully accepted as the expression of God's revelation to us.

I ran into deep trouble with my announcement that God had spoken to me. My family considered my claim and reacted instantly with an emphatic thumbs-down. You may know the story well, but you have not heard my side of it, and I represent the proverbial horse's mouth. I had a dream. Well, to be honest, I had two dreams with an identical meaning. As often happens in dreams, they mingled familiar sights and activities from the world around with unexpected twists and turns and a startling conclusion.

I was not looking for anything special. I was seventeen at the time, an impressionable age, but I was no stranger to teenage scepticism. I was working as a shepherd with my half-brothers, Dan, Naphtali, Gad and Asher, and I suppose I used to take frequent advantage of the fact that I meant far more to my father than they did (Gen 37:3). There was nothing intrinsically wonderful about me, contrary to what I believed then, but they were the sons of Bilhah and Zilpah, and my other half-brothers were the sons of Leah, whereas I was the son of Rachel whom my father loved much more than the other women he had taken as wives. I knew I had Jacob's ear, and I often manipulated him for my own ends, sneaking on my brothers if that could secure me an advantage over them (Gen 37:2). In an early reflection on those days, I realised that I must break the line of deceit which threatened to wreck our family by taking a permanent hold on succeeding generations. The favouritism I received from Jacob did not endear me to my brothers, as you'd expect from your own family life. 'When his brothers saw that their father loved him more than any of them, they hated him and could not speak a kind word to him' (Gen 37:4).

In my first dream, I was back at work. We were frantically busy at the time, and I must have fallen asleep at night with the fatigue of it all resurging in my dreams to reproduce the day's work. I began to dream of a field. Does this happen to you when you dream? You're fast asleep when a vivid experience breaks through your snores, which infuriate others, to convince you that you're wide awake. Next morning you groan in self-pity, 'I didn't sleep a wink all night.' But those who endured your noisy imitation of a donkey on the rampage either smile in mock sympathy or confront you with the truth, 'You had a perfect night's sleep—at our expense!' I don't think I snored too much, certainly not on this occasion, because my brothers would not have been slow to let me know if I had disturbed them.

In the field of my dreams I was at work with my brothers. That was no surprise to me and I felt quite at home. We were by no means the best of friends, and they ganged up on me whenever it suited them, but we worked together and agreed to differ. In my dream each of us was holding a sheaf in our hands. I remember the details so well after all these years that I find it hard to be sure that I was asleep at the time. We were binding our sheaves when suddenly mine jumped out of my hands as if it had come alive. I had to be dreaming, and I was. As my sheaf stood upright my brothers' sheaves left them to gather around mine, bowing down to it in reverent homage (Gen 37:7). Was this just a strange dream, or did it mean anything? Was God pointing me to my future? Perhaps the dream indicated the ruthless ambition of a cunning young man; perhaps God was lodging it in my sub-conscious memory so that I would hold on to his promise in the midst of devastating personal setbacks which were to come.

Now I know what you're itching to say. 'Joseph, hang on to this dream, but keep it to yourself; don't tell anyone about it, least of all your brothers.' I agree with you now, but I was only seventeen at the time, and you can't fix an old head on young shoulders. My dream was too exciting and I enjoyed its prospect too much to keep quiet about it. It might well rankle with my brothers if I told them, but that was a risk worth taking if it could put them in their places. In our day everyone shares their dreams and visions, and it never occurred to me to do anything else.

Later that day, when we were all together, I took the opportunity to tell my brothers. You had to grab any chance to be heard in the clamour, and I tried a quiet, nonchalant approach: 'I had an unusual dream last night.' Sometimes it worked; sometimes no one took any notice; this time it worked. They laughed at me but still wanted to know what I'd seen, and I spared them no details as I relished the audience. My dream went down like a lead balloon. Never mind what I thought of it, they knew immediately what I was suggesting to them. 'His brothers said to him, "Do you intend to reign over us? Will you actually rule us?" And they hated him all the more because of his dream and what he had said' (Gen 37:8). If one brother speaks to the others about a vision of their homage to him, he's asking for trouble, to say nothing of any sisters he might have. To be fair to them, I don't think it entered their heads to consider that God had been speaking through the dream. All they heard was an unpleasant description of a future they abhorred from a brother they despised.

ME!

Was it my fault that I had the dream? And what if God was speaking to me about my future? This dream was followed by a similar dream which included my parents in its scope. My mother was no longer alive, but the vision of the dream seemed timeless and pointed as much to her attitude to me in the past as it did to my future with the rest of the family. I have long since forgotten how far apart these two dreams were in time, but they were close enough to belong to the same period of family life, and to represent twin variations on a theme which was attractive to me but obnoxious to all my relatives.

I cannot recall how I appeared in this second dream. (You know how the most vivid of dreams has details which you lose before you wake up next morning.) I do remember that I was there, and I'm completely clear about my parents and brothers. Mum and Dad were visible as the moon and the sun, bright and imposing. I could almost feel the searing heat of the sun in my sleep, and I sweated in my bed. Eleven stars joined with the sun and the moon. They were not large, but they twinkled visibly in a dark sky. Imprinted on each star was the face of one of my brothers, each one clearly recognisable: Reuben, Simeon, Levi, Judah, Issachar, Zebulun, Dan, Naphtali, Gad, Asher and Benjamin. Once more, the point of the dream came in the bowing down to me of the sun, the moon and the eleven stars (Gen 37:9–10).

In the morning I was still shaking from this repeat version of an earlier dream. I was in no doubt about the reception awaiting me, but I never thought of keeping quiet. I think I hoped they would take me more seriously if they realised that the dream had been confirmed in a different form. Well, you're right, they did take me very seriously; they were furious! Even Dad turned on me, which was a rare discomfort. 'What is this dream you had? Will your mother and I and your brothers actually come and bow down to the ground before you?' (Gen 37:10). My brothers responded to me with hostile contempt, but my father thought carefully about my dreams. I had irritated him, but he wondered if there was more to it than the outrageous arrogance of a spoilt teenage son.

My dreams raised some intriguing questions. As time distances people from the events, they will find it easier to consider calmly my experiences. They may even come to marvel at the way God assured me of a future which was almost lost before it was finally realised.

The question of dreams

Does God speak to us through dreams? If he does, do we have the right to impose on others an experience which always arouses the suspicion that it's too subjective to take seriously? Can we ask others to believe that God is speaking in this strange way? Dreams are not subject to our rational faculties. They often contain elements of fantasy which lend colour to the air of unreality which surrounds them. They can be dangerous, leading the dreamer overboard in his acceptance of what he thinks they are saying. Dreams are risky ground for any action we try to impose on other people. No, this discussion is not futile or abstract. I am raising the question of two specific dreams I had when I was seventeen. I know that can be dismissed as an impressionable age, but older people than me have believed that God spoke to them in a dream, and I've not heard serious objections raised about them.

Abraham passed off Sarah as his sister, only to find that Abimelech, king of Gerar, fell in love with her and took her for his own partner. It was a dream which warned the king of the true relationship between Abraham and Sarah, and therefore of the dire consequences of his own conduct. 'But God came to Abimelech in a dream one night and said to him, "You are as good as dead because of the woman you have taken; she is a married woman" ' (Gen 20:3).

I'm not certain but I'm pretty confident that it's a

dream we're thinking of when Isaac, my grandfather, became convinced that God had spoken to him. 'That night the Lord appeared to him and said, "I am the God of your father Abraham. Do not be afraid, for I am with you; I will bless you and will increase the number of your descendants for the sake of my servant Abraham" ' (Gen 26:24).

My own father had a vivid and powerful dream. He was making the eager search which led him to find the beautiful Rachel as his wife. On the way, he stopped, overcome with weariness and hindered by a pitch-black night. Even with a stone for a pillow, Dad slept deeply (which is no surprise if you've lived in the same house with him), falling straight into a dream. 'He saw a stairway resting on the earth, with its top reaching to heaven, and the angels of God were ascending and descending on it' (Gen 28:12). In that vision he heard words and received promises which assured him of a mighty future, just as my dreams promised a great future. Jacob was moved as well as shaken when he woke. 'Surely the Lord is in this place and I was not aware of it' (Gen 28:16). But if you heard the words in your dream as Jacob did in his, you too would be impressed: 'I am with you and will watch over you wherever you go, and I will bring you back to this land. I will not leave you until I have done what I have promised you' (Gen 28:15).

My dreams landed me in distinguished company which provided me with worthy precedents for my belief that God uses such means to speak to us. I admit to you now that I was already nursing illusions of grandeur over my brothers because of my father's preferential treatment of me, and I could have concocted the dreams to help me realise the ambitions I held, but I didn't. Both of my dreams were totally genuine, whatever the cynics say. I saw pictures, I did not invent stories. You can't choose how you will dream and I had not pre-arranged the scenes which came to me in my sleep. Let's face it, it was my family who first put the dream interpretations into words when they reacted angrily against the apparent meaning of the visions I had described to them. Of course, we must be careful, proceeding with extreme caution if we want to insist that God uses dreams and similar visions to speak to us. But you're also treading on dangerous ground if you refuse to take seriously the kind of experience I have had. I suppose I am a bit defensive, but the matter caused me enough hot water to last a lifetime, and I paid in full for the blunders I committed in handling the whole affair. I still go round in circles when I try to reason out the subject, or had you already come to that conclusion?

I believe God spoke to me in two dreams; in fact my experience of dreams has all come in pairs, even when others have asked me for help in finding the meaning of their dreams, but perhaps that's a mere coincidence (Gen 40:5 ff; 41:25). He showed me a picture in my dreams. I held to the impression I had seen, sometimes firmly, sometimes by a thread so slender it seemed it must break, thus destroying all my remaining hopes. Those dreams reassured me in later suffering that there was a possible exit, I did have a future, and I was not trapped in a vicious cul-de-sac. If we are to be alive with the expectation of God's living word we must be open to the various means he uses to convey that word. We need to watch out for abuse of this openness, but I prefer thé risk of mistakes to the lifeless orthodoxy which has little enthusiasm for God's living action.

Why were two dreams more memorable, more compelling, more significant than all the others? Why is one man arrested in his sleep while another snores blissfully through the long night? Why do privileged dreams come from God to a spoilt child like me, but nightmares stalk those who want nothing more than a good night's rest? I simply do not know, all I can do is to tell you what happened to me without having the faintest idea why it happened. Maybe God loved me, and I know I never deserved that. My visions of the future could have warned me of suffering, betrayal and assault, all of which came to me in my adult years, but they didn't. I received pictures of authority and prestige to which I clung in my darkest times, although I had no evidence that my faith would ever be vindicated.

Others will also dream, and God will speak to them through the images they see in their sleep. These things will disturb an unimaginative mind and an envious spirit. Occasionally, dreams will come to sceptical victims who neither want nor seek such revelation, and they'll be embarrassed to admit, 'I've had a dream which I believe is from God.' It will do their humility a power of good, but their faith will profit even more. Of course, the interpretation of dreams will suffer some abuse, but dangers exist for almost everything we prize as sacred. Those who dream and hear from God will defy proud scoffers in an unusual witness to a God whose mischievous humour is as insistent as his freedom to choose how he communicates with men and women.

The handling of dreams

All right, I agree with you, I was stupid to tell my brothers. I should have waited until I was an old man. I see that now, as I reflect back on my life and share its lessons with you. But suppose I had never breathed a word about my dreams. Would it be convincing now if I took you through the mountains and valleys of my life and then quietly informed you that God gave me two dreams when I was a teenager which prepared me for the bitter setbacks which otherwise would have destroyed me? I doubt it, I can't stand smug people who ought to be surprised by events but sit there with an awful smile on their faces saying, 'I knew all the time that was going to happen.' And I never believe them! I think it's much more convincing for you and for me to have known that I began with a vivid promise which is not announced now as the illusion of an old man. What would you have done if you were me? When God deals powerfully with you, do you hide it away in your heart, waiting patiently for the right time to share it? Of course you don't. It might be better if you did, but what seventeen-year-old thinks like that or wants a wise, weather-beaten old head stuck on his brash teenage shoulders? Naturally, I would turn the clock back if I could, and if I could know then what I know now. If I could do that, I'd keep my dreams for personal assurance and for minimum publicity. But life is not like that, it's not full of seventeen-year-old centenarians, is it? (Gen 37:2; 50:22, 26.) And how many old man do restrain the airing of their wisdom with a dignified maturity?

Why should God speak to me? Not because I'm worthy, not because I'm highly gifted, but because he is God and chooses to do things his way. Perhaps he comes to me in dreams because I don't cope too well with intellectual information but I can manage visual aids. All I know is that I'm grateful and I've been humbled. Once I was proud, once I wanted everyone to know that I'd been chosen, but not anymore. I'd love to believe that God can entrust more to me because I've learned to handle it with a greater discretion that includes transparent humility.

When God speaks, I want to listen carefully in obedient faith. He doesn't speak merely to convey information but to summon us to active decision. The ultimate test of his word is that we act on our conviction that he has spoken, we don't sit back in enjoyment of the message. I made a serious mistake. I flaunted publicly a private communication which was intended to strengthen me for a dark future. Tragically, it fed a pride which preceded several nasty falls. The dreams are there for all time, and there's nothing I can do about it now. Our culture expects us to publicise our dreams. At seventeen, I was only too keen to do that, not least because the dreams sounded really exciting for me and they sorted out my brothers. But I've had many second thoughts since then about sensitivity to God and wisdom in the family. I presume people will quote me, refer to me, appeal to me and malign me. Some will be dreamers, others will be those who suffer from dreamers imposing an arrogant insistence, 'God told me in a dream, and that's it.' I believe that God spoke to me through dreams, and it's true to say that these were later vindicated in an amazing way. So far, so good. I've already made the point in addition that our culture expects such things to be widely shared. But I'm saying that I blew it in talking freely and proudly of my experiences. Whatever the culture expects, God was speaking to me for my private assurance, and I know, at least in retrospect, that I should have kept quiet. Vindication years later does not excuse an arrogant stupidity which upset my father and infuriated my brothers. If you do want to appeal to me for support, you have to be willing to share the fate which publication inflicted on me.

To tell or not to tell

I think it's all been said now, but will you forgive an old man who wants to be sure he's made his point? The question when God speaks to you is 'Why has God spoken to me?' You do need to know the purpose he had in mind when he addressed you. You'll often find that it's a private matter which can stay between the two of you. The trouble is that we're not good at keeping confidences, especially when sharing them guarantees the audience we crave.

In my dreams God was telling me about my future. As Abraham waited a quarter of a century for the fulfilment of the promise of Isaac, so I waited many years before my family became subject to my unique authority in Egypt, but the time did come. The dreams came to me to sustain me, not to warn my family. All they did for others was to stiffen resistance to me. The prophetic irony in my brothers' furious reactions illustrates the point that I must have been mad to say what I did. No brother or father could respond in any other way than mine did. I suppose that in a family of greater harmony than ours, one of them, almost certainly an older brother unthreatened by the pride of a younger, might have taken me on one side and whispered cautionary wisdom into my ear, but that was not likely with us. Such a gentle warning belongs to the role of a mother who loves her son enough to be honest with him but not so much that his foolishness blinds her; but my mother had died at the birth of Benjamin.

Dreams are only one way that God uses to speak to us, and we must keep the door open to every other way. Clumsy, noisy people can crush the willingness of wild life to make human contact. Similarly, we can blunder into the things of God and force him to withdraw whenever sensitive handling of delicate material is required of us, and we suffer great loss. I wish I had said nothing about my dreams. I wish I had kept God's word to myself. The message was for my faith, my comfort and my assurance that I would eventually be vindicated. I saw all that when I came to power in Egypt. I praised God for the dreams he had given me many years previously, and I asked him to forgive my stupidity.

Ponder carefully these aged reflections, and learn what to do when God singles you out to receive his word. The privilege carries a responsibility, not necessarily of keeping quiet but of handling rightly what he gives to you. Can you keep a confidence with God? Alternatively, do you have the courage for a public announcement if that's what he wants? That's often the time when you'd love to keep quiet. What you must do is to be sure what God is telling you, and then do it, no matter how hard it might be for you. In many ways, I wish I was still seventeen, but in others I'm content to be old. Bless me, please, by learning from my mistakes; but no, you'll insist on learning the hard way, as I did.

3

Grievous Bodily Harm

Our family was hampered from the beginning by its appalling start. Several decades of agony, hatred, remorse and bitterness passed before a dramatic expression of God's power produced an improvement. But what an improvement when it finally came! An incredible coincidence combined with a shattering discovery to lead to a moving reconciliation in a drama which took years to unfold.

I have already described how my brothers reacted to my dreams, but the birth of their ill-feeling towards me came a long time before that. We came from one father but several mothers. It was natural as well as inevitable that each of these women would vie ruthlessly with the others in the interests of her own sons. The fact that they were different mothers was far more significant to them than that they shared a common husband, Jacob. There is no more determined fighter than a woman committed to the advantage or protection of her son. Boys will be boys, and they will fight, but these petty conflicts are magnified as well as prolonged once mothers intervene with a biased involvement in a disagreement which otherwise would soon be settled.

My aunt was Leah, my mother's older sister. She gave birth to Reuben, Simeon, Levi, Judah, Issachar and Zebulun. Her servant was Zilpah whose sons were Gad and Asher. My mother was Rachel, and Benjamin and I were her sons. Her servant was Bilhah who gave birth to Dan and Naphtali (Gen 35:23–26). It's all rather complicated, but Leah's sons should have been my cousins as you can understand, but they also became my half-brothers because we all had Jacob for a father. As Leah's husband, I called him 'Uncle Jacob', but as Rachel's husband, I called him 'Dad'. I knew I was teasing him and this was a venture into sensitive territory which I never took when Mum was around; the joke did not amuse her! I escaped unpunished by my father for this cheeky defiance, but my cousins—sorry, my brothers—never tried their luck; in fact, the sons of Bilhah and Zilpah resented the way that my freedom to fool around was not open to them. I pretended to be confused by the ambiguity of our relationships, but I was winding up the adults who at this point lived on a very short fuse.

If only these women had realised that a protective, ambitious love, reserved solely for their own sons, was bound to create serious division in the family. Their own boys would suffer as much as any of the other sons. As striving women, they would also live in constant, jostling anxiety, fearing that a rival mother or son had stolen a march on them. The sad truth failed to pierce the walls of maternal determination which kept each of them lonely, vulnerable and suspicious. It prevented any united family life between us, and it multipled ill-feeling. We lacked a helpful sense of common identity through Jacob our mutual father, concentrating more on the separation of different mothers than on the unity of one father. We brothers, half-brothers to be more accurate, were strongly influenced by the antagonism between our mothers, and we made their divisions our own. Parenthood has been defined cynically as an acute form of insanity, and the definition fitted well in our case. The unfortunate consequence of this family strife was that we brothers tended to split quickly into rival groups according to the pressure on us of loyalty to our respective mothers—Rachel, Leah, Bilhah and Zilpah. Benjamin was young enough to be accepted by everyone, which put me regularly into a minority of one, an easy target when malice became physical.

My father's obvious favouritism towards me worsened the striving jealousy within our family. I enjoyed this at the time but now I regret it. It did bring me short-lived advantages, but also long-term misery. I have long believed that this favouritism from my dad was a direct result of my being a son of Rachel. I don't need anyone to remind me that there was nothing inherently attractive about me to secure the larger share of his attention, but he had longed for a son by Rachel, and I was that son. The other women were never more to him than tolerable alternatives, and it didn't help them that they were painfully aware of it. If arguments arose, Jacob listened only to my version of the story, and took my side. If there were presents, they came first to me. Dad had learned many trades in his concern for self-sufficient thriftiness, and one day he gave me a fabulous new coat (Gen 37:3). The colours were a riot, and the pattern was startling. There was no quiet walk for me once I wore it outside. I didn't speak, but I became loud. Frankly, I doubt very much if any of my brothers wanted the coat for himself. It was an embarrassment to me, but they loathed me for Jacob's favour which it represented. I traded shamelessly on my father's preferential treatment of me, capitalising selfishly on every little advantage I was able to wring from him. Gleefully, I dumped my brothers in trouble whenever I could, knowing that my story always won the verdict over their protestations of the truth. I was a nasty little boy, even worse than some of the nasty little boys who have pressed on me the misfortune of their company. I wasted no chances in my short-sighted conspiracy for preference, and big trouble piled up on the distant menu my brothers were preparing for me. Unwittingly, I stirred the ingredients they were mixing for my impending destruction. I cannot believe that this was entirely my fault, but I accept that I was the one who behaved as an obnoxious brother.

I blame my parents, as individuals and as partners. I blame the four women who should have sat down with Jacob and come to an honest recognition of the chaos they were inflicting on their sons through a selfish determination to promote their own offspring. But I was not a big enough person to refuse unjust privilege in order that others might receive fair treatment. Yes, I really would love to turn the clock back, but that is impossible. No man can do that, a lesson we learn the hard way.

My brothers had suffered prejudice; a mixture of deliberate discrimination, family injustice and parental bias had reduced their emotional security in the community where we lived. They watched closely the resentments which separated women who were thrown together in a strange relationship of partnership and rivalry. They knew they were a factor in the insoluble problem; innocent victims, but part of the problem. They were unsure of my father, and uncertainty with your dad always rocks the emotional boat. They needed no reminder that two brothers in particular, Benjamin and I, maintained a far stronger hold on our father's heart than they did. They were aware that he and Rachel had not hesitated in the past to deceive close relatives if personal advantage was at stake, and they feared that this would be repeated whenever their interests conflicted with mine or Rachel's. Her death at the birth of Benjamin freed them from part of their difficulty, but it aroused such sympathy for Benjamin that they had a fresh problem on their hands. Jacob always took Rachel's side in any argument among the women. This bred an aggressive insecurity in them which progressed quickly to fear. That fear did its own work in my brothers, producing a grudge which beat a sure path to physical violence, directed not against Benjamin but against me, his only full brother.

Jacob and Rachel could not inflict prejudice of this kind without creating a strong backlash. As each brother coped with his own feelings, he drew near to others who felt as he did. Soon, I was on the outside of an unspoken alliance whose bond was a burning jealousy of me. In talking together they shared their struggles and multiplied their grievances. The flower of active revenge is inevitable once you root a grudge in thought and water it with constant brooding.

I heard much of this story from my brothers years later. By that time they were duly humbled and ashamed of themselves, and we had enjoyed an incredible reunion in Egypt. I'd had plenty of time to ponder my selfish mistakes, and I saw clearly how I had asked for the trouble they gave me. I'd done more than ask for it, I had sat up and begged! Perhaps we were all victims of preceeding generations, but, at some point, each of us should have accepted responsibility for our own attitudes. I suspect that we all need some emotional healing which we can't handle alone, and the help should not be delayed longer than is necessary. Yet we mature through our acceptance of adult responsibility for our own lives. I could no more foist all the blame on cruel brothers than they could excuse themselves by appeals to a foolish father, cunning women and an objectionable little brother.

Talking recently with my brothers, they have acknowledged something I long suspected. It was only the lack of an ideal opportunity which delayed their retribution against me. My special coat and the account of my dreams had provoked them to pass a sentence which they waited to execute. The opportune moment came for these impatient men but I was blissfully ignorant of what lay in store for me (Gen 37:8, 18). They took a decision which was apparently spontaneous, but the verdict had really been agreed when my father made it obvious that my dream had irritated him. That freed them from all restraint or fear of paternal discipline—as if a dad who is cross wants his son murdered!

My brothers worked hard in the fields and they were expert shepherds. I presume I would have joined them in time, but my dad felt the anxiety which is typical of a man who fathers his children later in life than most men, and he held me back from adult responsibility. He worried about my safety in a way he had not worried about my older brothers, and they knew it. On one occasion, the sheep were grazing near Shechem, and my father knew roughly where they could be found (Gen 37:12–13). His decision to send me to visit my brothers dismayed me, but I knew the folly of protesting to a father I had recently angered. It would be easy to pretend to you now that I had a hunch that trouble was coming, but I know that's not true. I didn't want the heat and sheer hard work of a tiring journey to which I was still a total stranger. On the other hand, I felt no fear of my brothers because I was naively confident of their submissive obedience to my father. He commissioned me to check on my brothers and to bring him back a full report on their welfare. 'Go and see if all is well with your brothers and with the flocks, and bring word back to me' (Gen 37:14).

It was easy to find Shechem. The road itself was well beaten but I had to make a thorough search of the area before I came across my brothers. Fortunately, a local man helped me. He found me wandering around in the fields and asked me who I was looking for. He must have met my brothers who were pretty obvious as a large group of shepherds with an unusually large flock of sheep, because he remembered them well when I told him of my errand and asked him if he'd seen them. He had overheard them planning to travel on to Dothan. I hurried on to follow them and to complete my family mission (Gen 37:17).

When I left home to obey my father's instructions, I called out to him, 'See you soon.' We made no fuss about a parting which we expected to be brief. Neither he nor I could have dreamed that we would not meet again for so many years, and that when we did, I would be Prime Minister of Egypt with immense authority and all the resources of that country at my disposal. He and my brothers would be victims of a terrible famine, seeking help from a leader they assumed to be foreign. I often thought how casual our parting had been and how we would do many things differently if we had the slightest inkling of the future, even the immediate future.

My brothers could not believe their luck as I appeared on the horizon handing myself to them on a plate. Undoubtedly they had talked about me as they tended the sheep. They must have swopped ideas of possible fates for me, finding sadistic amusement in surpassing each other with evil suggestions. It wasn't brotherly fun, it was a malicious conspiracy for my destruction. They saw me before I saw them, and they just had time to agree their plan before I reached them (Gen 37:18).

The most popular suggestion was simple and brutal. 'Come now, let's kill him and throw him into one of these cisterns and say that a ferocious animal devoured him' (Gen 37:20). Their sarcastic humour showed that my dreams really had been the final straw for them: 'Then we'll see what comes of his dreams' (Gen 37:20). Reuben protested at their decision with the courage of an eldest brother. He was much older than I, and neither Jacob's favouritism of me nor my behaviour had ever threatened him. I suspect that he had a sneaking affection for me, but still found me unlikeable. His plea for my life came not from any lovely quality in me but from Reuben's pleasure in Dad's joy when Rachel produced sons for him in his older years. Reuben was a big enough man to be pleased for Jacob whatever it meant for himself. He pleaded with my other brothers to put me into a cistern without assaulting me but they were itching for my blood. ' "Let's not take his life," he said. "Don't shed any blood. Throw him into this cistern here in the desert, but don't lay a hand on him." Reuben said this to rescue him from them and take him back to his father' (Gen 37:21–22). There was no shortage of cisterns in the area. They are big holes which look like bottles sunk in the earth and they store water from the winter rains so that it is available for the dry summer. Anyone can easily fall into a cistern, and accidents often happen.

Reuben prevailed on my brothers, overcoming their grim reluctance to give in to him. They grudgingly agreed to follow his plan, and I suspect that some of them realised his intention of returning to rescue me. They stripped me of my notorious coat and threw me into the nearest cistern which, fortunately for me, was dry. I recall how they argued among themselves that this was a pointless violence on me which would bring them no benefit except the satisfaction of revenge. The argument lasted some time, and I just caught the sound of voices being raised and lowered in heated discussion. Meanwhile, a caravan group of traders appeared on the horizon. Dothan lies on a vital trade route which links the lands of the East to the South of Egypt. 'Their camels were loaded with spices, balm and myrrh, and they were on their way to take them down to Egypt' (Gen 37:25). In other words, they were trading in spices and medicines. Reuben was some distance from his brothers, attending to the needs of a sick sheep. Judah seized a mercenary initiative, urging on his brothers the folly of killing me. 'Come, let's sell him to the Ishmaelites and not lay our hands on him; after all, he is our brother, our own flesh and blood' (Gen 37:27). His brothers agreed, envisaging no difficulty in feigning my death to my father so that they could share the proceeds from the sale of a brother into slavery. That was the last they were to see of me for years, in fact they meant it to be

a final farewell. Reuben returned to the cistern and was terribly distressed to find it empty as well as dry. I had disappeared. My brothers maintained a pact of silence, and persuaded Reuben to accept the story prepared for my father which he himself half-believed to be true. 'Then they got Joseph's robe, slaughtered a goat and dipped the robe in the blood. They took the ornamented robe back to their father and said, "We found this. Examine it to see whether it is your son's robe" ' (Gen 37:31–32).

Only my brothers can explain how they coped with their callous deceit. It is for others to say what I deserved, but Jacob never deserved what they inflicted on him, however stupidly he had hurt them in his favouritism to me. Their news broke him, and I'm not sure that our reunion years later really produced a full recovery. I understand how much older he was by then, but something in him had died, as if he had realised his own folly too late to make amends, too late to prevent the tragedy he had suffered. I sense too my brother's regrets, but they know how impossible it is to roll back the years.

It may seem particularly cruel to you that my brothers returned my coat to Jacob after they had dipped it in animal's blood to give the impression that wild animals had torn me to pieces. There's no doubt that my father understood the message they intended to convey to him. 'He recognised it and said, "It is my son's robe! Some ferocious animal has devoured him. Joseph has surely been torn to pieces" ' (Gen 37:33). But this was more than a sick joke from wicked sons. My apparent remains were the legal evidence of my death, and brought Jacob to official acceptance that he would never see me again. His remaining duty was to confirm my death in a solemn ceremony which released my brothers from any liability in the matter. The legal process was designed to deal with livestock, but it could also cover the circumstances which seemed to be relevant in my case. How ironic that my blood-stained coat should help my father to free my brothers from any implication in my death. They accepted their freedom with obvious relish and dismissed me from their minds in a way that I never dismissed them from mine. My father grieved on, long after the customary mourning period. 'Then Jacob tore his clothes, put on sackcloth and mourned for his son many days. All his sons and daughters came to comfort him, but he refused to be comforted. "No," he said, "in mourning will I go down to the grave to my son" ' (Gen 37:34–35).

Another link had been forged in the chain of intrigue which bound our family. My brothers had piled up their lies as they hastily covered up the real circumstances of my death. Could one of us break that chain? Did any of us realise the guilt it laid upon us? Did we care enough to restore the damaged reputation of the Patriarchs? Or do we do no more than attribute everything to primitive days from which more civilised behaviour will emerge?

Looking back on it now, I see where we all went wrong, but I wish we could learn our lessons some easier way. I had wronged my brothers. They had suffered continuing injustice from my father, and they felt it deeply. Their resentment justified itself to them, as all jealousy believes itself to be reasonable. Once they had excused their grudge, they could go ahead with their 'no holds barred' revenge. But who then can break this destructive chain? Only the person who forgives, for where there has been great injury, there will be no healing until someone forgives. That was too difficult for my brothers at that stage of our lives, and it was scarcely easier for me many years later, but one of us had to take the only way left to us.

4

Come Lie with Me

I still shudder when I recall what happened, and worse still, what might have happened.

After my brothers drew back from killing me, they sold me into slavery and abandoned me to a fate in which they expected to take no further interest. Eventually, the Midianite traders sold me to Potiphar, a high-ranking official in Pharaoh's army (Gen 37:36). Potiphar's wife tried to seduce me in a clumsy attempt which combined cunning, persistence and crudity. When she failed she turned against me with vile accusations which were her ruthless response to my integrity. Potiphar had little choice but to believe his wife's story, although I still doubt that he really trusted her, and he threw me into prison as his wife lied her way into savage revenge on the slave who had spurned her advances. To be honest, it had not been so much an advance as a frantic charge, but it was a long time ago. I remember the moment when she first asked me to go to bed with her. It was a mixture of total shock, attractive possibility, stark fear and overwhelming pressure which a voice inside me suggested would be thoroughly enjoyable and permanently undetected. I suspect both suggestions were lies.

This woman was offering me something which found too willing a response in me and I dared not allow it to proceed. The temptation was awful but the stakes were my life. In my recollection of that terrible time, my memory flits from one to the other of the actors closely involved in the brief drama. I like to think that I have now forgiven a woman who was as unfortunate as she was evil, but the episode still hurts me deeply. Was this the road I had to take to remain in God's will? Does this mean that his sovereignty is always tinged with impotence? Or is the truth too complicated for my simple questions?

Potiphar

When a man buys you as his slave you have no idea what kind of person has paid money to own you. Slaves who have served several masters spoke of their own trembling apprehension, and warned me to watch for the eyes and laughs of potential masters. If a slave can strike it lucky, I did so with Potiphar. He was an honourable man with a justified reputation for fair dealing. He gave a good price for me, and he knew how to value his purchases. I often wondered how my captivity in his house could further the dreams which had promised me authority over my family, but such dreams had to lie dormant. I decided to put everything into my work, reckoning that this would stand me in good stead with a man as appreciative of careful work as Potiphar. Even in slavery I retained my ambition for a successful career. Resentful slaves suffer for their reluctance.

Potiphar trusted me. He noticed that I worked well and had enough intelligence to cope with routine domestic problems. I was 'above average'. Potiphar didn't take long to promote me in his household, and soon he appointed me as his personal attendant at home. 'Joseph found favour in his eyes and became his attendant' (Gen 39:4). This was a privileged and much envied promotion for me, or so it seemed at the time. Potiphar had boosted my standing considerably and I responded keenly to my additional responsibilities.

I quickly spotted that Potiphar was an adoring husband whose affection was accepted with insincere pleasure by his wife. I thought she used him. If other men were around her, her darting eyes were everywhere but on her husband. He valued her as a superbly attentive hostess, but I viewed her with suspicion as a dangerous flirt. I believe that my previous observation of this woman prepared me for the temptation which might otherwise have overcome me.

I was a normal healthy man, denied sexual love by my existence as a captive bachelor. It was not easy to resist an aristocratic woman who offered herself on the proverbial plate and whose favour in the house could be an extremely welcome advantage. It never entered my head to consider the consequences of her disfavour. But Potiphar trusted me, and he trusted his wife. Later, when she betrayed me with venomous spite, he acted far more leniently towards me than I could have expected. Why did he do that? Did he suspect her lies? Had this happened before? I don't know, but as far as I'm concerned he did not behave like an outraged husband. He was too calm, too quiet, too dignified. It's true he was angry (Gen 39:19), but it was a reserved anger; unruffled, decisive, but not outraged. I do not blame Potiphar for his treatment of me. I only blame him for making an unwise marriage which must have caused him nearly as much pain as it caused me.

Potiphar's wife

Potiphar's wife always accompanied him when he went to the slave market. She would cast a meticulous, hungry eye over the men her husband considered. I recall now how actively she advised him, leaving him in no doubt which slave she wanted. At the time, I thought she was offering him the benefit of her feminine intuition. Now I realise that it was lustful intention not loyal partnership which drove her on. I didn't question it at the time but I have wondered since why Potiphar was not suspicious of her close interest in slaves whose sole destiny was to perform menial domestic chores with which no self-respecting Egyptian would soil his hands. She knew already what I later discovered; she could manipulate any male slave she desired into a position of intimate availability in the house while her husband was away. Potiphar was putty in the hands of this scheming woman. He was more than conscientious and she despised his integrity, looking elsewhere for the casual pleasure which accepted lust as a substitute for love.

Potiphar's wife, I wish I could remember her name, was not that beautiful, but her sharp Egyptian features had their own appeal. Her attendants flattered her for the sake of their own survival and she held them in contempt but enjoyed their attention. Deep down she was a bored and frustrated woman. She lacked nothing, but nothing satisfied her. She knew how to use her sexuality to the most telling effect, tormenting men who were deprived of active married life. I was no more than the next available plaything, to be treated as a new toy which would amuse her until she was ready to throw it away in the search for further novelty. But I refused to be available. I was unwilling to co-operate with a pampered woman whose fury, when thwarted, took fearsome revenge.

Joseph

We look for advance, success, power and prestige, but when they come to us they often carry a sting in the tail. I fared well in Potiphar's house, gaining rapid promotion in the domestic hierarchy. Potiphar put me in charge of his household, and he entrusted everything he owned to my care (Gen 39:4, 6). I believe now, and I believed then, that

God was with me, although so much went disastrously wrong which I could not resolve. Here, I prospered (Gen 39:2). Now that I am an old man, I am not embarrassed to speak of my younger days as if they were the youth of another person. I was good looking and I knew it. I accept that you may find that hard to believe now, but I'm not too bad for my age, am I? I was aware of the scrutiny of a dangerous woman, and was flattered as well as wary. 'Joseph was well-built and handsome, and after a while his master's wife took notice of Joseph' (Gen 39:6–7). I gave my commitment to a master who often confided in me and treated me well. Potiphar trusted me because he was the kind of man who inspired loyalty in those who served him, proving to be extremely shrewd in his choice of men and extremely foolish in his choice of women. I wanted to demonstrate that I was worthy of his regard. Something of strong character and moral quality exuded from the man, challenging those around him to emulate their master. Potiphar's rapid rise to power in Pharaoh's army shows the good judgement of the Egyptian ruler. I wanted nothing more at that stage than to please the man who had restored my self-respect by his readiness to merge ownership with friendship. I also wanted to keep my head on my shoulders. The invitation to me was clear, 'Come to bed with me' (Gen 39:7), and I conquered it only because I had standards which I maintained in the face of relentless onslaught, irrespective of the cost to me of upholding them.

God

God had kept his eye on me. I might doubt that, but I never denied it. I viewed my promotion by Potiphar as a clear indication of God's blessing, and I attributed Potiphar's success to divine approval for his treatment of me. 'From the time he put him in charge of his household and of all that he owned, the Lord blessed the household of the

Egyptian because of Joseph' (Gen 39:5). How many men are as casual with their slaves as Potiphar appeared to be with me, although he did nothing that was not careful and deliberate? Many slaves never relax for one moment their alertness for an opportunity to escape. It overrides any personal loyalty they might feel to their master. Potiphar had assessed the risk with me, and he calculated that it was one worth taking. 'He did not concern himself with anything except the food he ate' (Gen 39:6). I think he was afraid of the secret addition of our more potent Hebrew dishes to his daily menu, and that was one risk too many for him. God was with me. I acknowledged him daily, and I told him how I felt, whether grateful for progress or resentful of slavery, using every opportunity for private prayer.

I'm not claiming that I was surprised, but one day Potiphar's wife summoned me. Apparently, longer-serving slaves than I fully understood the intention of her summons, but I was raw to the sexual intrigues of Egyptian mistresses, and I responded to her order as a slave to a mistress, not as a man to a woman. I expected further instructions from her, but she came quickly to the point and offered to have sex with me. I thought men were supposed to be immediate in their sexual appetites while women need more time to be ready for love. This woman was an exception. Her request was blunt, and I was stunned. I recoiled in obvious horror, and refused her. She knew by now that most men refused her initial advance, partly because they were afraid that it might be a cruel trap, and partly because they feared to take the very thing they most wanted once it was offered to them. She pressed herself on me, and the game of cat and mouse began. I refused her again. I made excuses. I backed out of the room, but she followed me. I protested my loyalty to her husband, pleading my religious convictions. 'With me in charge...my master does not concern himself with anything in the house; everything he owns he has entrusted to my care. No one is greater in this house than I am. My master has withheld nothing from me except you, because you are his wife. How then could I do such a wicked thing and sin against God?' (Gen 39:8–9). She sneered at me, looking alarmed for a fleeting moment which she failed to realise I had noticed.

This relentless woman would not be put off. She waved aside every objection. She had set her sights on a man she considered good-looking and desirable, and she was furious when he rejected her. This refusal was an unintentional insult on my part which she would not tolerate.

I dropped into bed that night exhausted, not from sexual antics but from spiritual weariness. The cost of remaining clean can be very high, as I was about to learn. The unrelenting pressure on me continued, day after day, and I nearly wilted under the heat she created. I did my daily work, and that was demanding enough, but she had an uncanny instinct for those times when she could corner me alone and renew her invitation, 'Come to bed with me.' I heard her words repeatedly, monotonously, in my sleep. They began to haunt me as much as they beckoned me. I dared not confide in anyone because they would be outraged and I could not hope to be believed. This woman knew every trick in the book, and she tried all of them on me.

Inevitably, she launched a fresh attack, and was it fresh! One day I went into the house to attend to my duties, but none of the household servants was inside. That was all she needed. She caught me by the cloak and said, 'Come to bed with me' (Gen 39:11–12). A woman was making a sexual assault on a man, but who would believe my story? She grabbed my clothes and tried to push me into her luxurious bedroom. Panic stricken, I tore myself from her and ran for it, anything to escape this nightmare. But the nightmare followed me. As I ran from her, she clung to my cloak, ripping part of it from me. I ran on blindly, frantic with horror as the possible

consequences of leaving some of my cloak in her hands hit me with brutal force.

I had no idea of the vengeance she would wreak on me for spurning her constant advances. She had my cloak, and she used it to twist the whole story: I had tried to seduce her; I had forced myself on her, fleeing the room only when she screamed for help; my cloak in her hands was proof of the rape I had attempted. She told her servants, repeating her accusations to Potiphar as soon as he arrived home. He gave me no chance to refute her and prove my innocence. Slaves are not innocent until proved guilty, they are just slaves. She who had lowered her voice to a deep, seductive whisper, 'Joseph,' now knew me only as 'that Hebrew slave' (Gen 39:17). Potiphar had no alternative but to react instantly, and he did his duty. 'When his master heard the story his wife told him, saying, "This is how your slave treated me," he burned with anger' (Gen 39:19). Something almost imperceptible in him flinched as she vented her fury on me. It is no more than a hunch on my part, but I don't think he believed her story, although his hands were tied. He, an Egyptian official, must accept the word of his wife against a Hebrew slave.

I can't have been her first victim. Maybe previous conquests had succumbed willingly to her offers, but no master can be unaware of sordid household rumours unless he's totally out of touch, and Potiphar was anything but naive. He had trusted me and he should have had me killed, but he spared my life. I'm grateful to him, but it doesn't add up to Egyptian methods of punishment. That's the reason why I suspect he was not too sure of his wife's indignant story. He had to take her seriously, but he let me off with prison, and a fairly gentle prison at that by the cruel standards of Egypt. Potiphar personally conducted me to my new home, a special enclosure reserved for the prisoners of the king. 'Joseph's master took him and put him in prison, the place where the king's prisoners were confined' (Gen 39:20). There I languished, until the next piece of my life's puzzle was fitted into place; but more of that later.

When God uses a man to great effect, it follows as surely as night follows day that he becomes a sitting target for physical temptation. It may come from his own active interest in a woman or from her initiative towards him, but it will come. There's no point in waiting until he's trapped in a furtive affair, gripped by an irresistible infatuation, or crushed by the disaster of a broken marriage. Sexual attraction is the well-tried ploy of a demonic enemy whose sole intention is to bring down the person who serves God and to end his effective work. You don't meet that by complacent piety but by constant vigilance. I dared not contemplate the pleasure she was holding out to me. I had to switch my mind, my desire and my eyes to something which was rightly mine, but I struggled. The deliberate provocation of a ruthless woman faced me, although sexual possibilities usually come with more subtlety than that. Both forms of temptation are hard to resist. Potiphar's wife offered herself to me so that I had no need of the crafty masculine tactic which wears down a woman's resistance. If I wanted the sin she offered me, it was there for the taking. On the other hand, the stupid woman provided her own deterrent to me with her brazen overtures. As a man, I preferred the encouragement of a good chase to meat offering itself on the slab. Her dress, perfume and female war-paint were all designed to kill, but they proved to be an overkill, and she became increasingly distasteful to me. A repeated offer from such a woman either overwhelms you or it becomes repugnant, and I was relieved to find shelter in the latter of these alternatives. I cannot boast to you that I kept clean by my inner purity or personal strength. I knew my own weakness, and it frightened me, but I did stand firm in the face of a terrible assault on my integrity.

It was a miracle of God's protection that kept me from sin with Potiphar's wife. Was anyone praying for me at that time? Did God ring warning bells which I heard and others failed to hear? I just don't know. I can't tell you why others have not been protected as I was. I saw all the possibilities. My body enjoyed the anticipation of hers and I trembled with the conflict of passion, temptation and resistance, but I found the strength to refuse her. She might have weakened my resolve but I managed to grow stronger. No man is immune from physical attraction, and illusions of holiness have preceded many a fall. The appeal this woman made to me would have been hard for anyone, let alone a frustrated slave with a reputation for his good looks and his physical power. I know how much my strong principles helped me in the crisis of personal conflict, and I spotted immediately the slippery slope which invited me to volunteer for my own destruction. The fact that God had spoken to me in my teenage dreams meant that I knew him, and I realised instinctively that this was not a private matter between a man and a woman, but a life under divine scrutiny. 'How then could I do such a wicked thing and sin against God?' (Gen 39:9). That is a discovery which other big names among our people will have to make for themselves (see 2 Samuel 12:13; Psalm 51). I shrank from violating the positive loyalty which I acknowledged to Potiphar and that made a real difference to me. He had trusted me, and I wanted to remain worthy of his confidence. If that's how you feel towards a man, you don't mess around with his wife. All this was at stake when the spiritual enemy launched his deadly onslaught. The more you serve God, the more you learn that sexual provocation is the chief weapon in that enemy's cunning armoury, and you haven't a hope of lasting the course unless you find the strength to keep yourself clean.

As far as Potiphar's wife is concerned, you should pity her as much as you blame her, but that is much easier to say now than it was at the time. Her dress, her speech and her movements oozed seduction, but there was something pathetic about her blatant promiscuity. She knew well what I have since realised; there are many ways of saying no, but only one way of meaning no. There were men before me who had refused her advances, but she found no difficulty in wearing down their resistance. She had spotted something in their initial rejection which said, 'No, but please try harder and you'll succeed.' It was all part of a sordid game they agreed to play together. I had to communicate to her, 'No, and there's nothing you can do to persuade me to say yes.' Sexually, that's hard for a man who prefers to hang on to his possibilities, but spiritually it is vital. It's all a matter of the signals which pass between two people, and you have to be more than careful if you want to continue as a trusted servant of God. We all need the kind of friends who will warn us, protect us and confront us before we fall, rather than comforting us after the tragedy has struck. The axe of sexual temptation hangs over our heads as a weapon which brings down many a man of God, but the expression of married love is a gift of unique beauty which the creative energy of God has offered to us. His forgiveness to those who do fall is an unmerited wonder, a light at the end of many dark tunnels, but the remorse on the way to that mercy is a costly price to pay for the brief pleasure of our indulgence.

I wanted to be honourable to God, to Potiphar, to his wife and to myself, and that proved expensive. With the benefit of hindsight, I'm sure that dishonour would have been even worse, but it's cripplingly difficult to suffer blatant injustice without growing bitter. The false accusations of a malicious woman damaged my reputation for years and I suffered a prison sentence I did not deserve. If I had protested my innocence too much I would have been punished even more for slanderous allegations against a woman of impeccable social standing. If only I could have established the truth. I stood no chance of winning, but my silence was hard, as it always is when you've been unjustly accused. I felt shamed, hurt, helpless and highly indignant. Sex-starved prisoners ridiculed me, revelling in nudges, winks and crude comments at my expense whenever they spotted a female in the course of our monotonous prison routine. They envied the passion with which they assumed I'd indulged myself, and it was pointless to protest my innocence to them. 'No smoke without fire,' they mocked, sure that the fire which raged uncontrollably in themselves was also burning in me. After all, what man in his right mind passes over the offer I received?

I have wished, occasionally, that I had taken her, but I'm relieved as well as happy that I stayed clean. If I lived in obedience to God, he would find his own way of vindicating me. How that would happen, when it would happen, I never knew; but I still hoped in my darkest hours that a brighter future would come because it had been promised to me in the dreams of my pampered youth.

5

Your Dream Has Meaning

It's no use complaining that you've heard enough about dreams. If you're reading about my life you need to follow the big stories, and I have some more dreams for you. I never sought a ministry in dreams, but people vote with their feet and I had to accept the anointing they foisted on to me. Thank you, I'm perfectly well aware that anointing comes from God, but once important men recognised a gift in me I had to conclude that God was at work again. I've learnt to read the signs, and I counsel you to do the same. My unsought fame as a Dreams Specialist became the means of my amazing rescue from prison, although it threatened to squeeze me further into the effeminate mould that my resentful brothers prepared for the spoilt youth whose arrival as a younger brother they had come to regret. They were burly shepherds who mocked me for behaving in a way they considered less than manly. But the tables would turn, and I'd show them that I was as tough as any of them.

I was faltering before God, and faltering badly. When my brothers assaulted me and threw me into the empty cistern, more disappointed about the waste of money than the loss of a brother, they abandoned me to the fate of a slave. They were supremely confident in their presumption that I had made my exit from their lives, and I suppose that, too, was my expectation. I had not fully grasped how they hated me, and it's difficult even now to put into words the despair I felt when the truth dawned on me. My father had spoilt me so much that I expected similar treatment from every adult I met. My brothers took great delight in smashing that out of me, and I lurched from one form of excessive desperation to another: fear, anger, humiliation and remorse for my arrogant stupidity in provoking men who were bigger and stronger than me. Scenes from boyhood flashed through my mind in a vivid playback of earlier years, and I shrank in horror at an obnoxious child unwittingly steering his brothers towards an active dislike which erupted into violence. But, you can't turn the clock back. My faith wavered as doubts crept in. No, to be honest with you, they flooded in, threatening to leave me without hope, without friends, without family and without God.

I've told you about my progress in Potiphar's house and that brought some healing to me as I tried to come to terms with my life. My rapid advance to responsibility reassured me that I had unusual abilities which an impartial man was recognising. I was an able worker and Potiphar lifted me as high as any slave could hope to rise. My spirits soared, my morale was high and I began to enjoy my work, without losing a burning desire for my freedom.

I screeched to an abrupt halt when Potiphar's wife betrayed me. 'This is how your slave treated me' (Gen 39:19), she lied to her husband and he took the action against me which he judged to be appropriate. That was the second time I'd been deliberately betrayed, and this was as much an assault on my integrity as on my freedom.

I loathed prison life. I was already a captive in Egypt, but to be a convict as well as a slave was more than I could bear. The prison routine made me realise how alien this country had become. The foul language of the prisoners was miles away from the cultured Egyptian I was learning in Potiphar's home and I barely understood what they were saying. When I did, I was sure that ignorance would have been bliss! I felt tainted with them, wondering if anything decent would ever touch my life again. At times like that you almost accept your own guilt, and I felt ashamed, not of what I had done, but of what others believed I had done. I had not sought the incident which implicated me in guilt whether or not I admitted it, and I knew in my heart that I was innocent. Fellow-prisoners, tormented by their own desires, taunted me, and I dreaded their abuse. I suppose they would have tired of their crude jokes if I had laughed with them, but amusement was the last thing I could find in my circumstances, still less in their knowing winks which followed me everywhere I went. They took it for granted that I was guilty, and they envied me the experience they believed I'd enjoyed. No one investigated the case and no civilised process found me guilty. The word of an aristocratic Egyptian was always sure to override that of a Hebrew slave. I had taken great pride in my personal appearance, and even that was used against me. The accusation was that my sole desire had been to be as eye-catching for the women as I could. I languished in Pharaoh's jail, sure that God never went prison-visiting, least of all in Egypt.

Somehow I clung to my faith in a personal destiny which my teenage dreams had promised me, but I no longer had a clue how they could be fulfilled. The flame was never snuffed out, although it dimmed to a very tentative flicker. I nursed hopes of renown, authority and public acknowledgement but saw no indication that anyone afforded me even a grain of respect. Was it no more than a dream? Was I suffering from the illusion of an intolerable pride? Had a lust for power consumed me? Thousands of people dream without attaching the remotest significance to the experience, except to believe, mistakenly, that they've had a bad night. Was I any different from them? Dare I mention in prison, 'God spoke to me years ago in two dreams. He promised me a distinguished future, and I still expect it to come true?' Perhaps they thought an Egyptian prison was a distinguished destiny for a mere Hebrew.

I had this strange ability to rise to the top wherever I found myself. It did not come from an outstanding education or academic brilliance; it was more basic than that. As some men are born to make money, I was born to rise. That made it hard for me to stay humble and hard to be popular, and both proved elusive to me. I grew impatient of men above me when I knew I could do a far better job than them. On reflection, we would do well to recognise that there are men—and perhaps one day it will also be possible for women—who emerge to prominence from every pack with a special capacity for leadership. We must free them by welcoming their obvious destiny which is bound up with ours, thus benefiting from the fulfilment of their potential. Even in the Egyptian prison I did well. 'But while Joseph was there in prison, the Lord was with him; he showed him kindness and granted him favour in the eyes of the prison warder. So the warder put Joseph in charge of all those held in the prison, and he was made responsible for all that was done there' (Gen 39:20–22).

I must have given clear evidence of being a born leader, and the promotion of a prisoner saved them the expense of additional staff. I may have been a natural leader of men, but it would be a long time before my brothers would concede that to me. It was part of my frustration in prison that I was aware of my potential but was only free to express it in a very restricted way. God had entrusted something to me which was more than a human talent, and I burned with impatience to put it all into action. Little did I know that his plan was working all the time, progressing steadily towards the time when every resource I had would be stretched to the limit. I see now that he wanted me ready in the right place at the right time. All I wish is that a more comfortable route had been available to me. But I think we have reached the point where I can tell you more about my ministry in dreams.

Pharaoh's cupbearer

In prison, I met a man who had been a cupbearer to Pharaoh. You'd probably know him as a butler, and I'll use both words for the sake of variety. We were together in this special enclosure I've mentioned which was reserved for the king's prisoners. There was an element of privilege about serving your sentence in this section of the premises but also one of acute danger, the danger of living close to the fickle whim of the king. While I was there, I met a mixture of highly interesting and very frightened people, of whom the cupbearer was one. I never discovered his name because names in prison represented a basic dignity which was denied to the prisoners. The butler had offended Pharaoh, although he refused to discuss the precise nature of his offence (Gen 40:1). I suspect it was something to do with royal drinks which found a mysterious and regular way into the butler's private quarters but I have no evidence for that suspicion other than the appearance of a man who had obviously drunk to excess throughout his life without any visible means of affording his indulgence. The drink must have fallen from the back of an Egyptian chariot.

The Egyptian court included many cosseted officials in a carefully guarded hierarchy. This was an unnecessary expense for Pharaoh but it flattered him in his manic need to outdo the monarchs of surrounding nations with an extravagant display of power and wealth. No employee, and no aspiring employee, wanted to lift any fingers to prune the work force because they knew what many powerful men forget; the redundancies one man initiates can run full circle, dispensing ruthlessly with his own services when the biter is bit. It's dangerous to live close to the king with your life always hanging on the slender thread of his unpredictable moods. The cupbearer had known his place in the court circle and he had abused it for his own advantage. Now he paid the price in prison.

My bitter experience with my brothers had taught me to watch men closely. I used to read faces and study movements and postures for any change of mood which might spell danger. One morning, I noticed that the butler and his friend, the baker, looked very upset. 'When Joseph came to them the next morning, he saw that they were dejected' (Gen 40:6). We often chatted together, although our mutual bitterness about prison life meant that we weren't good for each other. The butler's conversation was often near the bone, but he had a marvellous fund of palace stories which he told me with dire threats of personal violence if I ever repeated them. That was a pity because there's nothing like a good story for gaining the audience you crave. These were headline revelations based on his trusted insight into royal life, and I'm amazed that Pharaoh didn't execute him as soon as he was displeased. This man had real ammunition. There was no official secrets act in Egypt, only the danger of Pharaoh's revenge, but that was all that was needed. The butler's revelations would have ridden roughshod through any legislation which might have been passed.

I asked him why he looked so down in the mouth. 'Why are your faces so sad today?' (Gen 40:7). It was too early in the morning for any disaster to have distressed him but he answered me with pointed simplicity. He'd had a dream, a rare thing for him, which he felt certain was bound up with his future. But what was that future? The dream seemed to pose terrible alternatives: he was returning to favour with Pharaoh, or he was going to die, and he was scared.

I was not trying to be funny, but my reply was open to misunderstanding. 'Do not interpretations belong to God? Tell me your dream' (Gen 40:8). I was not suggesting that

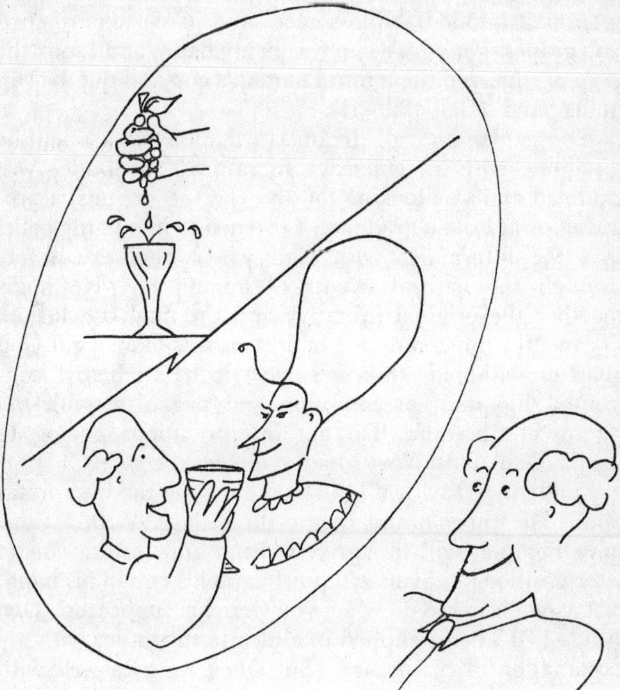

he could equate me with God, but it could have sounded like that. He told me his dream. 'In my dream I saw a vine in front of me, and on the vine were three branches. As soon as it budded, it blossomed, and its clusters ripened into grapes. Pharaoh's cup was in my hand, and I took the grapes, squeezed them into Pharaoh's cup and put the cup in his hand' (Gen 40:9–11).

The explanation of dreams in our day is a scientific discipline with an extensive literature. The butler was troubled and was looking for an expert in dreams; a professor, or at least a graduate. I listened to him in my belief that the future lies with God who works extensively through the natural events of human life. He holds together the original initiative and the final conclusion. For me, the understanding of dreams was more a gift God gives or withholds than a subject to be studied. I confronted Egyptian presumption and paganism with my rhetorical question, 'Do not interpretations belong to God?' (Gen 40:8). Now I had to deliver the goods.

Suddenly I saw it all, as God gave me the interpretation. 'The three branches are three days. Within three days Pharaoh will lift up your head and restore you to your position, and you will put Pharaoh's cup in his hand, just as you used to do when you were his cupbearer' (Gen 40:12–13). Then I slipped in a plea to the butler with my explanation of his dream: 'But when all goes well with you, remember me and show me kindness; mention me to Pharaoh and get me out of this prison' (Gen 40:14). At the time it seemed a marvellous idea, but now I know that I stepped out of God's timing in my attempt to seize the reins of my life, and I regret what I did. You can't manipulate God; he always knows what you're doing, but I wanted to force his hand to hurry on my behalf.

Pharaoh's baker

The butler was one of a pair, and his partner was a baker. They had served together in Pharaoh's palace, and both had fallen into disgrace. I suspect their offences were similar and that the baker's daily bread had cost him nothing for too long, but now he paid for it with his freedom. Knowing Egyptian bread as I do, that's an exorbitant price for a few loaves and I can't imagine why anyone would want to steal it, but I think that's what happened. I do not include their bread among the treasures of Egypt, and I never felt tempted to make off with it myself. Perhaps the baker mistook his daily loaf as a perk of the job, and Pharaoh evidently disagreed with him.

The baker also had his dream, and the details bore an uncanny resemblance to those of the cupbearer's dream; as if the same dream could guarantee an identical outcome for the unfortunate prisoners. The dreams weren't quite the same, but both were closely related to the daily work of the dreamer. As soon as the baker heard of my favourable explanation of the cupbearer's dream, he rushed to talk with me. I had spotted his early morning dejection, which surprised me because he was used to baking early and was usually the brightest man in the prison in those awful waking hours which spelt one more monotonous day for the inmates. Without checking for my attention, he launched into his story. 'I too had a dream: on my head were three baskets of bread. In the top basket were all kinds of baked goods for Pharaoh, but the birds were eating them out of the basket on my head' (Gen 40:16–17).

My words stuck in my throat as he spoke. I felt cold, dark and apprehensive as I saw his fate and I trembled to report faithfully what I had received for him. 'The three baskets are three days. Within three days Pharaoh will lift off your head and hang you on a tree. And the birds will eat away your flesh' (Gen 40:18–19). This explanation depressed me, let alone what it did to him. I felt excited for the butler, and hopeful for myself. I had asked him to

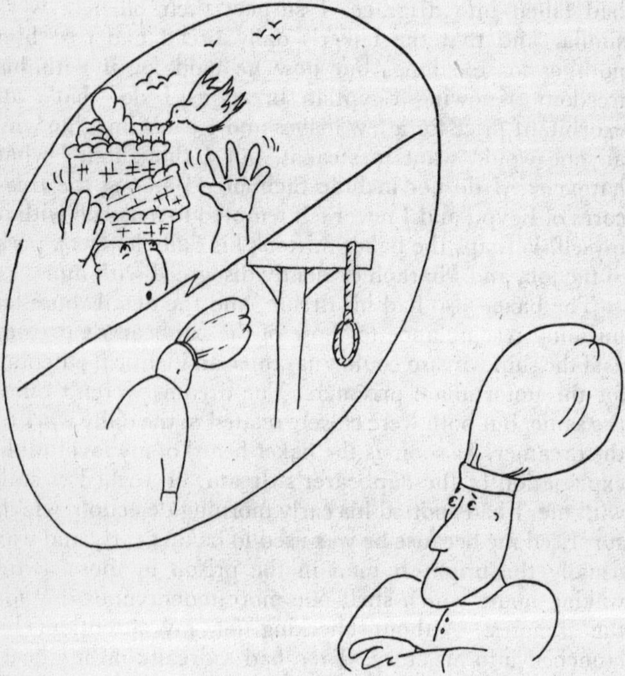

secure for me a fate similar to his own, but I didn't ask the same of the baker! The two explanations were as far from each other as the sun is from the moon. Both dreams could have carried a positive or negative meaning and I knew by then that the man who handles the things of God dare not presume on his word. Each question, each problem and each demand upon him is new and must be given a consideration which is genuinely open.

My words were fulfilled, and I took fresh hope that my own dreams might also be fulfilled. 'Now the third day was Pharaoh's birthday, and he gave a feast for all his officials. He lifted up the heads of the chief cupbearer and the chief baker in the presence of his officials: he restored the chief cupbearer to his position, so that he once again put the cup into Pharaoh's hand, but he hanged the chief baker, just as Joseph had said to them in his interpretation' (Gen 40:20–22). The head of each man was lifted up, one to live and the other to die. Do you see here a play on words? You can be lifted up in honour, and you can be lifted up to execution. The word 'lift up' can refer to glory or death. I wonder if it could ever mean both? (see John 3:14; 12:32). Of course, this may be idle speculation. We had a custom in those days where the one who sought the king stood or knelt with his head bowed, waiting for the one on the throne to take him under the chin and raise his head. All I can say is that for me, the play on words was deliberate.

Pharaoh

Meanwhile, Pharaoh slept peacefully at night, untroubled by his restoration of one man and execution of another. Both were unremarkable events in the pattern of life of an ancient Pharaoh. Lesser mortals were kept on their toes by the fear of having nothing on their shoulders! I don't know if Pharaoh had heard of the cupbearer's and baker's dreams, but I can't believe the cupbearer said nothing to him. I learned later that whatever he had said, the cupbearer made no plea for me. His own safety was the only thing on his mind, and he clutched selfishly at his new life. 'The chief cupbearer, however, did not remember Joseph; he forgot him' (Gen 40:23).

Two years passed and Pharaoh himself began to dream (Gen 41:1). He had two dreams which were in stark contrast to each other, but were also closely related. We are in fact dealing with one big dream which came to Pharaoh in two parts. I'm sure he realised that himself, and the awareness that they held clues to the future of Egypt led him to demand an accurate explanation. Every Pharaoh believes in his inherent right to halt the flow of national life if his dreams disturb him. Ordinary men just get on with the day's work.

'Pharaoh had a dream: He was standing by the Nile, when out of the river there came up seven cows, sleek and fat, and they grazed among the reeds. After them, seven other cows, ugly and gaunt, came up out of the Nile and stood beside those on the riverbank. And the cows that were ugly and gaunt ate up the seven sleek, fat cows. Then Pharaoh woke up' (Gen 41:1–4).

'He fell asleep again and had a second dream: Seven heads of corn, healthy and good, were growing on a single stalk. After them, seven other heads of corn sprouted—thin and scorched by the east wind. The thin heads of corn swallowed up the seven healthy, full heads. Then Pharaoh woke up; it had been a dream' (Gen 41:5–7).

Pharaoh would not rest until someone could tell him exactly what his dreams meant, and he paced restlessly round the room. He had a group of experts in the interpretation of dreams, most of whom conspired to be thoroughly professional, especially in their scale of fees. If you paid well enough, you secured the explanation you most wanted. A dream which indicated 'curse', could change its meaning if the price was right. I suspect that these experts had a good idea of the meaning of Pharaoh's dreams, but they were far too scared to tell him the truth. 'He sent for all the magicians and wise men of Egypt. Pharaoh told them his dreams, but no one could interpret them for him' (Gen 41:8). Strangely, the cupbearer's memory returned to him, and he gave the king his testimony, acknowledging my central place in it. He described me, flatteringly, as 'a young Hebrew' (Gen 41:12), thus enhancing my reputation in front of Pharaoh who sent for me. Frightened men rushed to obey a fickle ruler who held their lives in his hands. I knew better than to hurry my royal appearance, knowing that I had to turn up properly dressed for the occasion. I delayed the attendants while I washed, shaved and changed my clothes, gambling that Pharaoh would be more impressed than angry at my delayed arrival, but they chaffed, fearing an impatient tyrant. I haven't the faintest idea how I had access to a second wardrobe but I always knew how to capitalise on a favoured position, and I came eventually before Pharaoh (Gen 41:14).

I was tough enough to argue with Pharaoh until he satisfied me that he understood my position about the explanation of dreams. Pharaoh told me, 'I had a dream, and no one can interpret it. But I have heard it said of you that when you hear a dream you can interpret it.' I replied quickly, 'I cannot do it, but God will give Pharaoh the answer he desires' (Gen 41:15–16). The explanation I offered confirmed the suspicions of the court magicians in Egypt: the dreams were related, with a vicious sting in their tails. 'The dreams of Pharaoh are one and the same. God has revealed to Pharaoh what he is about to do. The seven good cows are seven years, and the seven good heads of corn are seven years; it is one and the same dream. The seven lean, ugly cows that came up afterwards are seven years, and so are the seven worthless ears of corn scorched by the east wind: They are seven years of famine...Seven years of great abundance are coming throughout the land of Egypt, but seven years of famine will follow them. Then all the abundance in Egypt will be forgotten, and the famine will ravage the land.... The reason the dream was given to Pharaoh in two forms is that the matter has been firmly decided by God, and God will do it soon' (Gen 41:25–27, 29–30, 32).

Suddenly I saw another chance; this could mean more than freedom. A new horizon suggested itself to me, beckoning me if I had the courage to go for it, and I was never lacking in nerve. I laid my trap and sprang it on Pharaoh, warning him of seven years of plenty followed by seven years of terrible famine. Then I pressed my subtle claim: 'And now let Pharaoh look for a discerning and wise man and put him in charge of the land of Egypt' (Gen 41:33). He obliged me as he went through the motions of consultation, as all good dictators and wise ministers do. 'The plan seemed good to Pharaoh and to all his officials. So Pharaoh asked them, "Can we find anyone like this man, one in whom is the spirit of God?" ' (Gen 41:37–38). He offered his suggestion in such a way that everyone knew it was the announcement of my appointment, and no one argued against me.

I had impressive terms of employment, and Pharaoh spelt them out in public. 'You shall be in charge of my palace, and all my people are to submit to your orders. Only with respect to the throne will I be greater than you... I hereby put you in charge of the whole land of Egypt' (Gen 41:40–41). I knew I wasn't dreaming when I felt him press his own ring on my finger and I smiled to myself when it flapped around. His podgy little hands had much fatter fingers than mine, but I thought it would be pushing my luck too far if I had the ring altered.

Pharaoh presented me with a luxury uniform, a company vehicle and free mileage. I rode in a chariot as his second-in-command, and men shouted before me, 'Make way,' (Gen 41:43). I was really the originator of the 'Make Way' march, and if I had had sufficient foresight I would have copyrighted the whole idea and made a fortune. My word was not to be questioned, and all the land would honour me. Pharaoh appreciated the explanation of his dreams and there were rumours that he'd gone over the top in his excessive delegation, but I wasn't complaining. I took all he gave me, believing that my dreams of long ago were beginning to find fulfilment, and I determined to remember his precise words, 'I am Pharaoh, but without your word no one will lift hand or foot in all Egypt' (Gen 41:44).

I have used the years to ponder the office I held in Egypt. I am no expert in the interpretation of dreams. I have not written books to publicise my secrets or my methods, and I never tried to cash in on my success. God worked through me at one time in my life, and I tried to respond fully to him. Where did I find the confidence to declare what I felt inside? What if events had proved me wrong? What is the interpretation of dreams anyway? Yes, there are unanswered questions about these primitive stories, and sceptical minds will hesitate to make use of them, to their lasting detriment.

There is no need to hide from reality just because you want to live close to God, and I was not spared the harsher side of life. My brothers abused me, a privileged woman betrayed me and her husband dumped me in a foreign jail. That does not suggest a flight from reality into some fanciful religious experience lacking substance or relevance. I was a man grappling with his faith who desperately wanted to avoid the gnawing emptiness which threatened to swamp every religious conviction I held. I drew near to God in prayer where I sensed images and saw pictures. These did not appear by coincidence, they came when I pleaded with him to speak to me—anything but silence. He set the agenda, retaining the authority over my life which I had previously given to him. I learned to trust those impressions because they came as specific answers which in time were vindicated. They guided me and confirmed my faith, harmonising with accepted spiritual truth and leading me into a positive ministry which enriched the growing circle of those who asked for my help. These experiences of God included my ability to explain dreams, but they were part of something bigger. They allowed me the freedom to consult friends without rushing me into hasty action. Of course, I had plenty of dreams which had no apparent meaning, and I often told those who came to me that their dream meant nothing as far as I was concerned. I refused to pretend that I had something to offer unless I really did, and I spoke only when something definite urged me to help those who were puzzled or distressed. There were times when people went away more anxious than when they'd arrived. Remember the Egyptian baker!

6

Feed the Hungry

Pharaoh's dream warned us of famine which I made explicit in my explanation of the dream which I believed to be God's way of speaking urgently to Egypt. But would we take any notice of the warning? Pharaoh responded instantly by putting everything into my hands. There was an element of the ostrich who buries his head in the sand, but there was also shrewd wisdom in what he did. On the one hand, he wanted to leave the real headaches to me, and on the other hand, he wanted me to carry the can if my interpretation of his dream wasn't fulfilled. At the same time, he recognised that I was the right man for the job if my outspoken predictions came true. God communicated his word through the sleep of a pagan king, challenging me to a new way of life and weighing me in the balances.

I knew that God was testing me. It was easy to insist that I believed in him. Most people I have met claim that, but it makes no obvious difference to the way they live. When Pharaoh summoned me, appointed me and delegated all authority to me, my credibility was at stake. The sole reason for the radical change in my life and the national outlook of Egypt was my certainty that God had spoken to us through Pharaoh's dream. Only people who are willing to stake their reputation on evidence which appears to be flimsy, but is rock-solid to the eye of faith, can nope to see God work in great power. The majority live in a deadly scepticism which professes faith but risks nothing. Despite his native unbelief in our God, Pharaoh heeded my warning. I thought a lot about that, and I have used him as a provocative example to those who ought to be far ahead of an Egyptian king in their surrender of faith to our Hebrew God. The response of unbelievers will regularly shame the scornful apathy of those whose familiarity with God breeds contempt for his demand (see Matthew 8:10). Pharaoh listened to me as none of Noah's contemporaries listened to him (Gen 6:1 ff).

We had to act quickly. God had revealed himself to us through his word which unleashed a demand for prompt action. I meet a lot of people who think that when God does speak, he's handing out a hard message which takes all the fun out of life, but that is a tragic mistake. The best thing we can ever do is to respond willingly when he calls us to obey him because he is acting in our best interests. We may not see it that way at first; our obedience may seem costly, forcing us into decisions which sift our priorities, but decisive obedience is always the best offering we can make to God.

I had to lead Egypt into the obedience of today. Tomorrow would bring a new demand. I discovered that the emphatic preference was to 'take it easy and let's see how things go', but I knew how things would go. God had made himself perfectly clear, and every wasted day of the next seven years would demand a penalty in human life. He was calling us to make decisions not to enjoy discussions, and the most important word for us was 'now'. The word which spells apathy is the word 'sometime'. Too many people knew that we'd have to do something about Pharaoh's dream 'sometime', but I wanted to do it 'now'. It was too easy to take for granted the annual coming and going of the seasons. We had suffered bad harvests and enjoyed good ones, and we had come to terms with the inevitable uncertainty of it all. But we were not facing the alternative of good or bad harvests, we were moving from seven years of unprecedented plenty into seven years of devastating crop failures. The one chance we had of survival lay in our immediate obedience to God today and not tomorrow, now and not sometime. It was my awesome responsibility to initiative an effective programme.

I had to motivate Egypt into fullscale action to save her own life. This salvation would not appear for several years, and there was no possibility of an early vindication for my policy. Only God could vindicate me personally, and that was bound to be a long way off. I needed to enthuse the people by goading them into a willing acceptance of the national plan for their survival. The danger I faced was one we all face, of putting off until tomorrow what we know we must do today. Every day mattered, a precious gift which I refused to waste.

I was thirty years old when I entered the service of Pharaoh king of Egypt (Gen 41:46). This was an ideal age to begin a new work. As I stepped into the public limelight I felt there was something prophetic about being thirty. The demands of Egyptian captivity helped me to mature quickly, also revealing my boundless energy. Some pitied me for the burden I carried, but I revelled in the enormous challenge of a job I loved. At an earlier age I'm sure I would have blown it, not least in my handling of the older men who were under my authority. As an older man, I would have lacked the necessary stamina for the endless travelling, the hectic chasing around and the constant cajoling of those whose work had to be consistent and reliable if my plan was to stand any chance of success. At the age of thirty I felt right for the job, and I was raring to start work. The danger involved and the faith which motivated me gave me the rare blessing of total job-satisfaction.

I was frantically busy, but I found time to become a husband and a father. Pharaoh gave me the name Zaphenath-Paneah and honoured me with the gift of Asenath, the daughter of Potiphera, priest of On, as my wife (Gen 41:45). Before the years of famine fell on us, Asenath and I had two sons, Manasseh and Ephraim. I made no secret of the meaning of the boy's names which I felt were an important commentary on our circumstances. Manasseh was so named 'Because God has made me forget all my trouble and all my father's household' (Gen 41:51). Ephraim's name had a lovely meaning, 'God has made me fruitful in the land of my suffering' (Gen 41:52). These family joys completed my temporary transformation into an Egyptian, but strange events were looming on the distant horizon to return me to my Hebrew roots.

The records mention me by name: 'Joseph went out from Pharaoh's presence'; 'Joseph collected all the food produced'; 'Joseph stored up huge quantities of corn'; 'Pharaoh told all the Egyptians, "Go to Joseph and do what he tells you to do" ' (Gen 41:46, 48, 49, 55). It was as true then as it is today that it is the man at the top who takes the accolades in success and the brickbats in failure. These are the unchanging terms of leadership, and you can't have the former if you won't have the latter. I accepted from the beginning that the buck stopped with me at all times.

It was obvious to me that we needed a vast organisation to support the programme I had in mind. The project was simple—'Food for the Nation'. Many men gave themselves to me as responsible and loyal colleagues, and our work-force grew daily. I was ruthless with anyone found to be lazy or corrupt because I knew I had to nip all trouble in the bud. We wanted every sack of grain we could harvest, and I urged on the Egyptians a total commitment to the plan of rescue. If I found a man of quality, I hung on to him, signing him up for service and shifting him regularly so that he gained a full knowledge of the scale of our business. I chose my staff and stuck with my own decisions. As soon as I trusted a man, I released him to pick his team and decide its method of operation. We needed buildings, transport and constant communication between the various departments. We issued regular bulletins of progress so that we held the enthusiasm of a nation which otherwise would quickly flag. Of course, there were occasional murmurs, petty resentments and minor rebellions. I treated these as both natural and inevitable, which freed me to be unruffled when they were drawn to my attention. I dealt openly with known problems without taking much notice of troublesome rumours. If I heard of unhappiness I sent important colleagues to the source of the difficulty, insisting that they listened carefully to the grievances. The high priority I gave to those who were genuinely disturbed was enough to dispel most of the likely outbreaks of discontent. Fires which began to smoulder received immediate attention, and I had men ready to douse the flames. The people realised that I had created an efficient machinery to troubleshoot their complaints, and this reassured them of my concern which in itself calmed most of the storms which threatened us.

I gathered from my mistakes that people responded well when they fully understood what we were doing, and I formed a network of gifted people who relayed explanations, progress reports and forecasts to the most far-flung corners of the country as well as the main centres of population. I reckon this was a very early exercise in public relations, and it worked well. We had our scoffers who were sceptical of the famine warnings I had sounded, and they pointed out the abundant harvests which accompanied my grim warnings. Their contempt made me mad, but I enjoyed asking them whether or not I had correctly forecast the wonderful years of plenty which were preceding the famine I expected. The doubters influenced a few people who couldn't look beyond their noses, but my solemn announcement of seven bad years to come; my careful argument that the stores insured us against those years; my assurance that the food would be freely distributed if I was proved wrong; and my threat that those who took no part in the collection of food for seven years would eat none of it when scarcity fell on us, was enough to win the day. Trouble-makers work in the dark, with the illusion of secrecy. Wherever I found them, I flushed them out and challenged them to repeat in public what they'd been muttering in private. Very few of them took me up on the challenge, and those who did rarely lasted long.

'The seven years of abundance in Egypt came to an end' (Gen 41:53). The time we had dreaded arrived. We had worked frantically to store as much food as we could, and we were as ready as any people could have been for the approaching ordeal. We requisitioned old buildings for emergency use as grainstores. We rushed up new buildings in a massive programme to beat the famine. Egyptians swarmed like ants over newly created building sites which multiplied all over the land, and the food poured in. It looked too much, but I squashed every hint of complacency as an extremely dangerous luxury we dare not afford. The discipline of my emergency measures had already been justified because no one in Egypt could remember one harvest as plentiful as any of the seven consecutive years we enjoyed, and I did not hesitate to remind them, 'I told you so.' Now the harsh times were on us, of which it was also true, 'I told you so.'

It was a long time since we had looked beyond our national concerns, seven years to be precise. If you are preoccupied with your own life, you lose your wider interests. Pharaoh's stomach for conquest had gone, and he feared no invasion. He had always been wary of an enemy infiltration over the north-eastern frontier which he tried to prevent by garrisons and a wall, but now he had survival and not war on his mind. He maintained close contact with me, checking our progress and congratulating himself that this Hebrew was an inspired choice for Prime Minister. In this way he retained some of the glory while I did the work. The critics were silent, even those who bitterly resented my dramatic rise to power. Events were vindicating me, but I was hardly excited. A few cynics accused me of putting a curse on Pharaoh. They were not convinced that I had brought God's word through my dream explanations, but my position was strong enough to put down their opposition. Pharaoh had vested such authority in me that I could handle them without reference to him, and they were very careful what they insinuated and where they spread their trouble; Pharaoh always stood behind Joseph. I was content to ignore them, secure in the place I held in Egypt.

The famine years were awful in Egypt, but they were worse elsewhere. 'There was famine in all the other lands, but in the whole land of Egypt there was food' (Gen 41:54). This was the time I had been waiting for as appeals began to flood in from all sides. 'When all Egypt began to feel the famine, the people cried to Pharaoh for food. Then Pharaoh told all the Egyptians, "Go to Joseph and do what he tells you" ' (Gen 41:55). 'And all the countries came to Egypt to buy corn from Joseph because the famine was severe in all the world' (Gen 41:57). I held on patiently until the need began to bite. I had decided to delay any distribution of food until the national mood had changed from selfish greed to realistic simplicity. I thought it would do the Egyptian stomach good to reduce its notorious appetite. Once people understood my policy, they accepted what I was doing, and deprivation improved their priorities. Then my system went into operation; selling measured rations, preserving family records, and assessing local needs. Black markets made a brief appearance, but I had been waiting for them and was ready to crush them before they took a firm grip anywhere. My refusal to show mercy to the early offenders

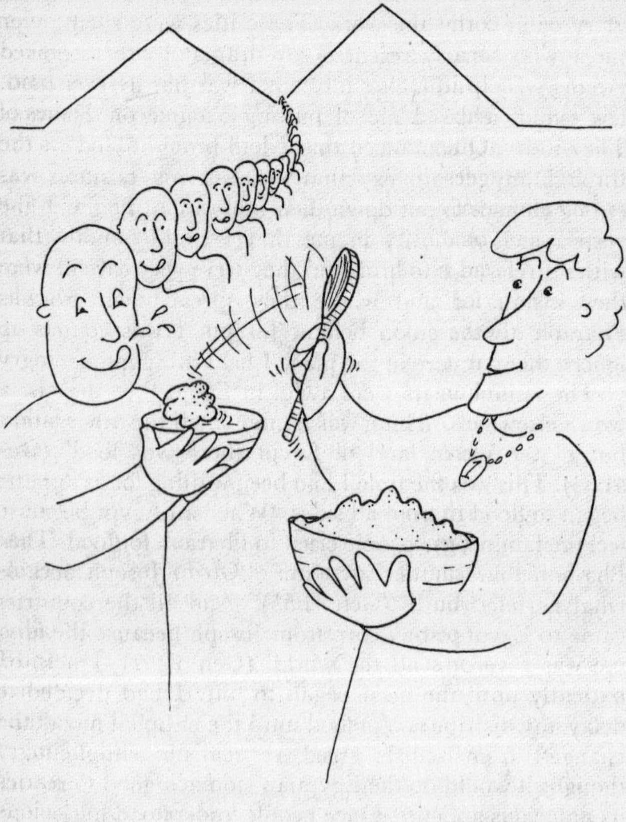

proved to be an effective deterrent, and I'm confident that the food did reach hungry bellies at fair prices.

News of corn in Egypt spread rapidly, and a popular saying was born. Countries around Egypt had long looked to her for help in famine, because she was a fertile land, but local neighbours suffered with life among the stones of hill country. Queues formed as people swarmed across the borders, refugees in all but name. My immediate task was to take notice of this hungry invasion and to deal with the reactions of some Egyptians to it. They were resentful that people who had taken no action in the years of plenty were now begging for our help. But the appeal made to us was not made on the basis of merit but of need, and it was up to me to hear them or reject them; they were hungry people, and hunger feels the same whether you are a deserving case or not. In fairness, we must admit that those who lived outside Egypt had not received the warnings which circulated our country, they didn't have the dreamers in high places that we had! The mean response went round Egypt, 'Charity begins at home.' That enraged me because I was not concerned with the beginning of charity but with its destination.

Too many people around us were suffering badly, countless horror stories were travelling the rounds, and I had no time for petty nationalism. We had a clear choice in front of us: to open our hearts or to close them, and the battle was on for the conscience of Egypt. Hungry foreigners had not prepared as we had, and their granaries were empty not overflowing. It's true that their previous laughter was rebounding on them, and many of them must have known about the massive taxation by which we levied a high proportion of the annual harvest from every farmer in the land for seven years. Few of them had missed the joke at Egyptian expense about a people who gave literal obedience to a word from a God they didn't honour through a dream they couldn't verify, but now it was verified before their own eyes. Too late they faced their own folly as they suffered at the brink of starvation.

I wrestled with this appeal from starving people. Our resources were limited, but the hungry crowds made an obvious claim upon us. It was not appropriate to hold a conference about the merits of their case, because they were hungry and we had food. The only question was, would we let them have anything to eat? We couldn't wait to check for a surplus, they were asking for immediate and sacrificial action, for the redistribution of our food so that more could benefit from the supplies. God was involved in all this. He pressed principles of responsibility on me which demanded more than I had expected to face, and I squirmed with the responsibility which was mine. He was claiming every area of my life, and I couldn't be content anymore with offering correct sacrifices on appointed days. I fought and argued, protesting that the fate of countries around us could not be my concern, and all he seemed to say to me was 'these people are hungry'. My satisfaction at the end of seven good years vanished as satisfaction before God usually does, and my heart would not rest while I kept people locked outside it.

Unknown to me, my father heard news of corn in Egypt. Impatient as ever, he rebuked his lethargic sons, their energy sapped by a poor diet. 'Why do you just keep looking at each other?' (Gen 42:1). Then he dropped a broad hint which soon became a firm order. 'I have heard that there is grain in Egypt. Go down there and buy some for us, so that we may live and not die' (Gen 42:2). They had stopped eating home-produced mutton which became increasingly scraggy as the famine took hold. They were convinced that things must improve soon, and wanted a remnant of the flock to be the basis for a new beginning when better times returned. Ten brothers were goaded into action, much against their will. They had stomachs for food, but not for a long journey. Reluctantly, my brothers set out for Egypt, leaving my father at home with his young favourite, Benjamin, who had replaced the Joseph they believed to be dead. 'Jacob did not send Benjamin with the others, because he was afraid that harm might come to him' (Gen 42:4). None of them had an inkling of what lay in store for us all, and I was no better informed than they were, except that I did know I was still alive!

The thought had often crossed my mind, what will happen if my family comes to Egypt for food and I meet them? I reckoned that the chances of this happening were extremely remote because we had so many distribution centres, each with its own staff. It would need a remarkable coincidence because I did no more than tour the centres to ensure things were running smoothly; Prime Ministers did not often roll up their sleeves in Egypt. But I still wondered, and I examined every crowd. I fantasised on the remote chance of a family reunion, but my saner moments insisted that it would require a major miracle for me to find my family. I asked myself, how I would react if I did meet them, but I had no idea of the answer. You can never tell how you will respond to circumstances of emotional pressure, but once the possibility was raised in my mind, it stayed with me. I tried to dismiss a thought which refused to go away.

I thought long and hard about our granaries stacked high with corn. They looked enormous—the original food mountains—but they were not there for waste or for the artificial preservation of high prices. They helped us to meet human need. I was proud of our achievement in storing so much with so little antagonism from thrifty Egyptian farmers who felt keenly the loss of their independence. Once they caught the vision I shared with them by strenuous publicity, they outdid each other in their enthusiasm for multiple stockpiling. Their pride made them possessive, and they knew how quickly stocks could run down. Now further demand faced them from hungry neighbours. The activity in Egypt had aroused considerable curiosity, and pressure grew on us to be merciful with our abundance rather than sparing with an unpredictable surplus. Pressing needs were forcing plentiful harvests out of all memory as the famine stretched itself before us. Seven years of hardship are much longer than seven years of plenty.

By careful planning we divided our stocks into years and months, rationing the distribution accordingly. I made regular checks through loyal officers whose surprise visits to unsuspecting granaries maintained local honesty. We cut off losses to the black markets which were an outlet we refused to tolerate, and I was excited that we succeeded as quickly as we did. I allowed no one to outwit me or to bribe me out of integrity.

Egypt survived, existing more than living, but others slowly starved, turning to us in their desperate need. They thought of nothing but food, and were ready to pay any price, suffer any indignity, go to any lengths, if only we would provide them with food to take home. Humiliated, they grovelled before us. Even Egypt could not hope to supply this crowd, and I watched as the nation hardened its heart to an emotional appeal which was calculated to weaken all resistance. I faced a question I could neither postpone nor duck: did I accept any responsibility for those in need merely because they were in need? I concluded that I did. The questions burned into me; they were my own questions, and I was tough on myself. 'How big is your heart?' 'How far do you look?' 'Will you change the system to include those who are excluded?' 'Must the hungry wait for the chance of a surplus when they need help now, or they'll die?' 'Will you sprinkle your unwanted grain on the graves of those whose cries went unheeded because you weren't sure if there was enough for Egypt, but now there is a surplus?'

I squirmed under this examination, and I made my decision. I admitted the hungry crowds to the corn of

Egypt on the same terms as our own people, and I accepted the controversy of my action. I drew my defence from the answers I gave to my own questions, while my critics complained that my faith shouldn't become tangled with politics and social concerns. Their purity of faith would have preserved food for Egypt, and let the nations die in their own neglect. But I was responsible for those who cried out to me. I was not choosing them, they were choosing me because I had the resources to save them. If we shared what we had, we would all live; if we kept what we wanted, we would prosper and they would die. They appealed to me, not from a shared language, a similar culture, a common religion or from mutual good will. They appealed to me from their need.

These are early days for awkward questions, and you may feel wearied by them, but I'm not willing to spare you the crisis of responsibility which I had to face. I wanted to postpone difficult things for an easier time but they wouldn't leave me in peace once they'd grabbed my attention.

Meanwhile, my brothers travelled to Egypt. None of us was prepared for what was coming, but God was making me ready to give them a good hearing and to have some fun. I can only believe, looking back, that he still planned to fulfil my dreams.

7

The Use of Power

The fact that I became such a powerful man in Egypt has made me think about the way men handle power—as yet that opportunity is not open to women. My early dreams told of power, power over my brothers and my parents. The premature death of my mother had put her beyond the reach of their fulfilment, but they must have posed a serious threat to the rest of my family. Neither my brothers nor my father enjoyed the prospect I held out to them, and my brothers hoped that their assault on me would prevent me from ever realising my obvious ambitions.

But I did come to power, in Egypt. Having lived as a captive under the tyrannical Pharaoh, I tasted the wine of supreme authority in his land when I found unexpected favour with him. I have already told you exactly what he said to me, 'You shall be in charge of my palace, and all my people are to submit to your orders. Only with respect to the throne will I be greater than you' (Gen 41:40). Forgive me for repeating myself, but even now the words are ringing in my ears.

It's my amazing rise to such power which has forced me to think carefully about its use. I had my teenage visions, as you know, but their fulfilment in adult life has far exceeded their extravagant promises—I was going to say, 'has far exceeded my wildest dreams!' I have been a powerful man. Others have wanted my friendship, my company, my smile, my eyes and my ears. They have also wanted my downfall, my job, and even my life. They wish me well, hoping that they can ride in the vanguard of my triumph, and they hope I crash, so that they can replace me. Men crave power; they plot for it, kill for it, sell everything for it—even their souls—and they willingly betray friends and principles if they see power within their grasp. If you become powerful, you lose all chance of making impartial friendships. Yes, I am listening to your protests; you can take an honourable path to power; you can exercise it with real integrity, but if you do, you belong to a very rare breed.

I think my observations are worth making because of my unusual experience. I was a bitter young man transformed into the first minister in Egypt; a slave who became the statesman Pharaoh entrusted with unprecedented authority, and you don't have much time to prepare yourself when that happens overnight.

Let's look at some of the aspects of power which have affected me most deeply.

The surprise of power

The path to power rarely runs straight. I did not shine academically, nor did I have the advantage of a privileged family. My progress did not take me to an outstanding job by which I attracted the attention of those above me and secured a place in their ranks as a springboard to the ultimate heights. That would have been too easy. I travelled to power along a road with dramatic twists and turns and a lot of big potholes! I was lifted up, and I was thrown down. In my family home, in Potiphar's house, and in Pharaoh's prison, I rose and fell. I made no bid for power, but one day I woke up as an ordinary man—in fact, a slave and a convicted rapist—and I went to bed at night with power in my hands that was almost absolute.

I had nothing welcome on my horizon, only the prospect of public disgrace and hard labour, but God surprised me, keeping to the assurance of my dreams which proved to be signposts to my future. He thrust me forward and I took my chances. The personal earthquakes which had devastated me failed to destroy me, and I did not forget where the signposts were pointing. I don't think it was a question of losing and regaining a distant goal. It was more a matter of a fantastic surprise from God. I was going up and down in a way that made no sense to me at all, but perfect sense to him. Only my dreams gave me a chance to understand my life, otherwise I was completely baffled. Wherever I went, I gained power, and that made me think carefully about my destiny. But the power always fell out of my hands as quickly as it had come to me. Often I saw no exit from a bitter predicament; then a way out would come, just at the right time. Power fell into my hands, and men followed the lead I gave. It dropped into my lap in a way which seemed arbitrary as I watched others scheming vainly for the positions freely offered to me. I was amused to overtake on the inside those who were struggling desperately to stay in the fast lane. If you give yourself to God, you have to be prepared for his surprises. Your road to power won't take the shortest distance between two points, it will suffer dead-ends and cut back on itself; it will wander aimlessly and deceive cruelly, but it can hit the fast straight without warning of a dramatic change of speed—at least, that's how it was with me. If God works in your life, he chooses the route and the speed, and you'd better be ready for anything. If you don't see things that way, all I can say is, that's how power has come to me, through circumstances which have made me rueful as well as humble.

The enjoyment of power

I relished the freedom which power gave me to make my own decisions and steer my own ship. When we set up the famine programme in Egypt, I chose collecting points and storage units, I put men into leadership and dismissed those who failed, and I had full authority to respond to my family when they arrived in Egypt to buy corn.

When I worked for Potiphar, I established the daily routine, and he held me responsible for the other servants who had not expected to answer to a fellow-slave. I enjoyed that limited independence. Even in the Egyptian prison, after my apparent disgrace with Potiphar's wife, I gained power over fellow-prisoners.

I discovered that I thrived on pressure; not crushing pressure, but enough to stimulate me and set the adrenalin flowing. I didn't carry a clip-board with its mark of empty importance, but I wanted to keep busy. Others relied on me because I ruled their rise or fall, and I never treated that lightly. Decision-making was not something which terrified me, as it does some people, because I knew that decisions solve problems rather than create them. A man's attitude to decision-making is a sure indication of his potential to reach the top. If he hesitates and fudges, he hasn't got what it takes. The lesser man, not at all lacking in intelligence, dithers while his decisive colleague responds eagerly to every dilemma, cutting through the difficulty with a firm decision and pressing on to the next obstacle. I made up my mind from the start that I would give decisive leadership so that everyone knew where they were with me. I know that has added to my enjoyment of power and taken a great deal of the strain out of it. The position I held in Egypt brought me responsibility, freedom, independence and some control of my own destiny, and I loved every minute of it. Now I understand why most men cling to power long after their effective contribution is over, although I'm not justifying their selfishness. They know that the moment they resign they'll lose the privileges of power, and few of them are big enough to take that step. We who take power should not hide behind the pretence that we're shouldering the burden of high office for the benefit of others, because they are themselves coveting our alleged burden too much to be grateful, and they are more than willing to take over, if only we'd step aside.

The responsibility of power

Throughout seven years of bumper harvests I was always aware that a fickle Egypt and her moody Pharaoh would clamour for my head as soon as anyone starved to death in the seven famine years which followed the plenty. The buck stopped with me. Crafty as ever, Pharaoh had seen to it that I and not he was responsible.

While in Potiphar's house, I knew that he would summon me if there were any hitches in the smooth running of the home. It was his choice to trust a Hebrew immigrant, but he argued that he had delegated power to me and I was therefore accountable to him, very convenient logic for my Egyptian master! I enjoyed the power, but I had to have answers ready at any time.

I could have learned my trade by watching others, but I would have picked up some very dubious standards. Power makes its own searching examination of personal integrity because it is more likely to be misused than well used. You call the tune when you have power, and others follow your lead. They adjust their principles to accommodate the trends you set, because they see that as their only way of survival with you. I imposed a domestic morality on Potiphar's house until his wife betrayed me, and everyone knew I would not tolerate any compromise of high standards.

It was the same when I became Pharaoh's chief minister. I set the moral tone. The ethics of Egypt came from the ethics of government which was in my hands.

Unscrupulous people assumed that they could establish a black market for corn. They anticipated rich profits and were confident of persuading me to turn a blind eye to their operations, taking it for granted that I would protect them from exposure if they rewarded me well enough. Within days they were ruefully aware that I was not looking to enforce the death penalty, but those found guilty of corruption in these days of terrible human need were putting their own lives at risk if I caught them. I was not susceptible to bribery or threat, and some discovered this to their cost. The nation was trusting me for its life, a deposit of confidence which I took seriously, and I gave everything to respond worthily. Beyond Pharaoh, and beyond all Egypt, I saw God and recognised that I was accountable to him. Pharaoh had given me authority, but God was the ultimate source of all power and I answered to him.

The exercise of power

If you occupy the seat of power and start work the next day, what are you going to do? Power is not something abstract, it is a practical exercise with many lives at stake. I had an officer's house to run. No one beyond Potiphar's circle cared about his house, but it became my world and part of the world of those who lived in it. Our dramas and headaches meant nothing to anyone but his family, his friends and his servants. The emergencies which cropped up only disturbed those for whom the name 'Potiphar' was significant. But the exercise of power in his house meant daily action and long hours of work for me.

When we had those marvellous years of harvests in Egypt, I organised the campaign to store food ready for the barren years we were expecting. As soon as they came, I took charge of the food distribution. Others watched me, wondering, 'How does Joseph exercise power?' They were looking for signs of weakness or tyranny. They were probing for strengths and for possibilities of their own advantage, but I knew what they were doing. They felt they must remain in my favour because I exercised power. I pretended to be blissfully unaware of all this but I kept my eyes and ears open, a vital necessity for every good leader who values his own skin. We Hebrews must always stay one step ahead of the Egyptians.

I could easily have hugged power selfishly to myself, with plenty of examples among my predecessors in authority, but I treated my position as a solemn trust I dared not betray, and I took careful thought for the next day. The rising generation was expecting ready-trained leaders, men who were fit to wield power, and I was keen to prepare successors for my high calling. Pharaoh had other ideas. He saw me as a necessary one-off, almost a necessary evil, and he had no plans for establishing a permanent role over which I exercised a continuing influence. Wise farmers insist, 'Farm as if you're going to farm for ever,' and I wanted to do that with the power I held in Egypt.

The temptation of power

If you have aspired to the heights of power, its temptations will multiply around you like flies swarming to consume anything in their path: the temptation to abuse those who want your favour, to oppress those who can't answer you back or refuse your demands, to unload blame on to defenceless juniors whenever things go wrong, to silence your critics, to regard power as a licence for your own extravagance, to keep a tight hold on national purse-strings which maintain the structures of your power and to indulge in the sexual excesses which accompany most tyrants. I wanted to be known as a consistent, humane man who overcame these temptations and held for myself the high ideals which I expected of everyone else, but it

wasn't always easy. The temptations of power were real, and I felt them.

Those who pleaded for food, once it was known that Egypt had corn, confronted me with temptation. I've already mentioned the inner struggle I faced over that. Part of it lay in the fact that everyone knew the decision was mine; there was no hiding-place for me. I could adopt a generous policy: disposing of our surplus as soon as I was confident that we had enough, easing back on our own consumption in a sacrificial concern for foreign need, accepting responsibility for anyone who was hungry and rescuing them from starvation although they would still be short of food in the midst of our adequate supplies. A generous policy could take many forms, and the temptation was to choose a line of action which would appear humanitarian but would also retain most popularity in Egypt where any discontent could easily gather pace and wipe me out.

There were those who encouraged my willingness to feed a wider world than Egypt, and even in Egypt itself many felt I had made a valuable contribution to peaceful co-existence. Little did they realise how I had struggled within myself with the options before me. Few wanted to accept my suggestion that we should teach the neighbouring countries how to feed themselves so that they were no longer dependent on us in times of shortage. Egyptians enjoyed this useful reliance on us into which others had fallen, and had no desire to see it go. It is a big temptation to hold people in your power once they're there, and it's hard to resist. I knew I must make the attempt. We sold food and people stayed alive, but the poor remained poor, the hungry remained hungry, and the dependent still depended. I was a good man while I perpetuated the system, and a dangerous trouble-maker when I questioned it. While we helped people but failed to free them, I doubted the value of the help we gave; it wasn't costing us enough.

These aspects of power fermented in my mind after my early dreams combined with my wildest fantasies in a fulfilment which surpassed anything I could have expected. When two years of the famine had passed, I met my brothers in a reunion they did not realise until I announced myself to them, reminding them also of our serious plight, 'For two years now there has been famine in the land, and for the next five years there will not be ploughing and reaping' (Gen 45:6).

I was on duty at one of the food stations, planning to assess procedures for the sale of corn to foreign visitors who sought our help. I was disturbed by my previous reluctance to allow food to cross from our borders until I was sure we would survive ourselves, and I wanted to make amends for my selfish inclinations. I suppose, in retrospect, that I also wanted to be around if Hebrews came to us just in case my brothers made the journey; after all, my father might still be alive!

My reputation always went before me and I could never catch people unprepared for my visits. However much I tried to keep the human touch, most people treated me with an anxious deference because that was the response they had learned to powerful men. They all knew that I held their lives in my hands because of my own position and the influence I had on the ear of Pharaoh. No foreigner would dare to stand up when he greeted me.

When a group of Hebrew men did arrive, they fell to their knees as soon as they realised who I was, the chief minister of all Egypt. The truth hit me like a bolt from the blue, 'These are my brothers!' I didn't recognise any particular brother, I just knew it was them. A wave of emotion swept over me, completely destroying my composure which I struggled to regain. I covered up as well as I could by squashing any visible trace of welcome, pleasure or gentleness, and men who have tried hard to conceal their own feelings will recognise a familiar masculine tactic. 'As soon as Joseph saw his brothers, he recognised them, but he pretended to be a stranger and spoke harshly to them' (Gen 42:7). I had no fear of them realising who I was, because the possibility that I was alive, let alone in front of them with such authority, could not have entered their heads. I quickly relaxed enough to talk with them, subjecting them to a thorough interrogation. As I did so, I played for time and my mind worked feverishly on a plan to deal with these nervous, unsuspecting visitors. I had planned for years what I would do in these circumstances but I'd never reckoned with my own emotions, and I was determined to play my cards right. I wanted the trumps as well as the aces. My dreams flooded back, strengthening me to give my brothers a tough time. I was in power now, and they would feel the rough end of my tongue; I would make them tremble under my authority before I let them off the hook. It was difficult to do it with a straight face, but I managed my part well with an angry accusation, 'You are spies...you have come to see where our land is unprotected' (Gen 42:9, 12). I don't know how I stopped myself laughing, and we all had a good laugh much later when the full story came out.

I was playing with hungry men who protested their innocence with obvious horror. ' "No, my lord," they answered. "Your servants have come to buy food. We are all sons of one man. Your servants are honest men, not spies" ' (Gen 42:10). Unwittingly, they volunteered their family history to a man whose identity would stun them. 'Your servants were twelve brothers, the sons of one man, who lives in the land of Canaan. The youngest is now with our father, and one is no more' (Gen 42:13). They told me what I longed to hear, my dad was still alive, and they dismissed the chief minister of Egypt in five words, 'And one is no more.' If only they knew!

I used my position to impose my will on my brothers. I could not ignore the mention of Benjamin at home. He had stayed behind with my father, but I demanded his presence in Egypt, and they had to do what I said. Once I had decided how to treat them, I wasted no time in offering my brothers a deal. That should have warned them that they were dealing with a Hebrew and not an Egyptian! I was holding one of them in Egypt while they could take corn home and bring Benjamin back to me. I was very specific in the terms I laid down. 'If you are honest men, let one of your brothers stay here in prison, while the rest of you go and take grain back for your starving households. But you must bring your youngest brother to me, so that your words may be verified and that you may not die' (Gen 42:19–20). I listened carefully as they shared their dismay, innocently confessing the guilt they felt for the way they had treated me all those years ago. 'Surely we are being punished because of our brother. We saw how distressed he was when he pleaded with us for his life, but we would not listen; that's why this distress has come upon us' (Gen 42:21). I had used an interpreter to maintain the pretence that I was a native Egyptian, so they were quite happy to speak Hebrew in front of me with no idea that I understood every word they said (Gen 42:23). I listened, amused, as Reuben dissociated himself from their crime. 'Didn't I tell you not to sin against the boy? But you wouldn't listen! Now we must give an accounting for his blood' (Gen 42:22). This was painful as well as funny to me, and I was losing the battle to control myself. I needed time, not least to compose myself and I asked them to leave me, detaining Simeon when the others left for home. With mischievous cunning, I gave orders to fill their bags with grain, to put each man's silver back in his sack, and to give them provisions for their journey. Once I'd done this for them, they loaded their grain on their donkeys and made for home.

I never knew what happened to my brothers when they discovered the money, but they must have been quite as scared as they were excited. Their pleasure in obtaining free food from the Egyptians of all people would have been tempered by a worrying suspicion that this was a deliberate trap. Sometime later they did tell me the full story but they refused point-blank to say anything about finding the money in their sacks. The matter deeply embarrassed them, and I hung back from teasing them about it; but I was itching to pull their legs.

Apparently, my father was distressed as well as angry when his sons arrived home without Simeon. It was even worse when they announced the deal I had forced upon them to bring Benjamin to Egypt. 'Jacob said to them, "You have deprived me of my children. Joseph is no more and Simeon is no more, and now you want to take Benjamin. Everything is against me" ' (Gen 42:36). Reuben pleaded with the old man, offering his own sons as sacrificial hostages for Benjamin's safe return, but my father was typically stubborn. 'My son will not go down there with you; his brother is dead and he is the only one left. If harm comes to him on the journey you are taking, you will bring my grey head down to the grave in sorrow' (Gen 42:38). Only the increasing bite of the famine persuaded him to change his mind. 'Now the famine was still severe in the land. So when they had eaten all the grain they had brought from Egypt, their father said to them, "Go back and buy us a little more food" ' (Gen 43:1–2). It's amazing how you can influence a man if you lean on his stomach!

Back in Egypt, I had no idea of what was going on between my brothers and my dad, although a few shrewd guesses about the old man's tantrums were not likely to be far wrong. One day the news was flashed to me that the Hebrew visitors were back. I had kept their identity a total secret because I took the view that the only way of keeping an important confidence was to tell no one. When I set eyes on Benjamin, it nearly broke me on the spot, but I made a frantic effort to hide my feelings. I couldn't believe how much he'd grown since I last saw him, but you try telling any young man, 'My, how you've grown,' and you're asking for trouble. I had no intention of ruining our reunion with stupid thoughtlessness, and in any case it was too early to throw off my Egyptian disguise.

I ordered a state banquet, a provocative extravagance in such a serious famine and a risky use of my position. 'Take these men to my house, slaughter an animal and prepare dinner; they are to eat with me at noon' (Gen 43:16). I ignored the angry reactions around me, pretending not to see my brothers' apprehension. They held secret discussions with my assistants as they floundered for their lives, and I hid my awareness of their discomfort. I was still not ready to renounce all revenge. We treated them as honoured guests, but they remained tense, wondering if they were the real sacrificial victims. A steward led them into my house, gave them water to wash their feet, and provided fodder for their donkeys. When I joined them for the meal I couldn't resist a sly question about my father; at least I asked them about their father: 'How is your aged father you told me about? Is he still living?' (Gen 43:27). I questioned them about Benjamin: 'Is this your youngest brother, the one you told me about?' (Gen 43:29). Without waiting for their reply, I spoke to Benjamin. No one will ever know what those few words of renewed contact meant to me. 'God be gracious to you, my son' (Gen 43:29). I called him 'my son', and that was a fitting word in our respective positions, but I longed to say, 'my brother'.

The time had now come when my yearning for reunion overcame my determination to keep my family dangling on a piece of string. I had enjoyed the initiative which my power gave me, but I was ready to grasp something which I had feared might never come to me. I was going to tell my brothers that Joseph's dreams had come true.

8

Reunion, Remorse and Reconciliation

I have learned to proceed with great caution when I'm living under emotional pressure, and meal-times have often given me valuable time to think. I found this especially helpful when I had to cope with meeting my brothers, particularly Benjamin.

I longed to identify myself to them, although in many ways they were now total strangers to me. We'd had years apart, and my life had become bound up with the fate of Egypt. We had never known each other well because our mutual dislike had prevented us from drawing close to each other. Their implacable hostility to me united them, while I was separated from them through my father's favouritism which I had milked greedily for every possible benefit. I lost my brothers because I behaved so stupidly towards them.

We were all together, but I ordered the servants to serve our food separately. If only my brothers had recognised the voice of authority which barked its instructions, 'Serve the food' (Gen 43:31). I decided to let the Egyptian custom take its natural course. The servants served me by myself, my brothers by themselves and the Egyptians who ate with us by themselves, because Egyptians refuse to eat with Hebrews. We must have looked a ridiculous sight, having a meal together but eating separately! It's ironic to me that Egyptians have strong scruples about eating with Hebrews. 'Egyptians could not eat with Hebrews, for that is detestable to Egyptians' (Gen 43:32). I see among our own people a growing feeling that we are the ones who should be separated from others for meals, and I suspect the whole idea stems from a negative reaction to the Egyptian practice. This may prove to be one of the most retrograde steps a people can take, for it is in eating together that we bring down the barriers between us, and in refusing to do so that we reinforce them in position. You can't allow religious scruples anymore than national prejudice to divide one group of people from another, but I see it happening and it's not a healthy sign.

For the time being, however, I accepted the Egyptian custom, chief minister though I was. Blood is thicker than water, and I was being pulled towards my brothers, but shock waves were about to ripple through Egypt as the dignitaries around me showed horror and astonishment at the personal attention I gave to these foreigners. Their warm welcome into my house was the final straw for those I had already offended by my inexplicable departure from normal conduct (Gen 43:16–17). I wanted my brothers to see the kind of place in which I was living. These privileged quarters went with my job, and were rather different from the permanent home they had planned for me in a desert cistern, although both were rent-free. I was terribly moved at the sight of Benjamin after all these years, and I had to rush out to find somewhere where I could burst into tears without public embarrassment. I went into my private room and wept there. Then I gave my face a good wash, pulled myself together and issued firm instructions, 'Serve the food' (Gen 43:30–31).

I saw to it that Benjamin was treated with favour, although I don't know now what made me do that, except perhaps that he was the only full brother I had. 'When portions were served to them...Benjamin's portion was five times as much as anyone else's' (Gen 43:34). I was not likely to endear him to his brothers any more than my father endeared me to them when he showed me similar favouritism all those years ago. I was perpetuating Dad's short-sighted folly, as sons are prone to do. Benjamin however, was too busy demolishing the food on his plate to worry about the envious reactions of ten famished brothers.

There was one final trick up my sleeve. Strangely, I was convinced that once my brothers knew who I really was, I would lose my hold on them. Whatever had gone before; whatever authority my position in Egypt gave me; whatever national dignity I had, they would reduce me to 'young Joseph', and no brother can remain in awe of 'young Joseph'. I decided to prolong their agony, and mine. This time I would make them grovel and squirm and plead. I would plunge in the knife for one last twist in the family wound.

I was playing with power and with years of bitterness for which I blamed my brothers. Things had turned out well for me, but that was no thanks to them. I could feel this resentment easing itself away from me but I was determined to indulge it one more time before I let it go for ever. My brothers still hadn't a clue that I was Joseph, and they had no alternative but to play the game my way, which was all the better for me. I planned to strike at them through Benjamin and their fear of my father's special love for a son who had two irrefutable claims on his heart: he was the youngest son, always a privileged position in the eyes of an older dad; everyone (except me) believed him to be the only living son of the woman Jacob loved above all others, Rachel. Benjamin ruled my father's heart, and the rest of my brothers offered Dad a loyalty of fear and honour which pandered to his selfish ways. I was looking for a final display of power over them to flaunt my position and satisfy my thirst for revenge. I'm not proud of my behaviour, and all I can plead is that you understand how much my feelings were in turmoil as love and hatred, bitterness and forgiveness, revenge and mercy all jostled together for priority.

I instructed my steward to fill the sack of each Hebrew with food, and return his money to him, as on the previous occasion when they had travelled to Egypt. In addition I wanted him to put my personal cup, a priceless example of Egyptian silverware, into Benjamin's sack. I didn't name him as 'Benjamin' to the steward because he was already suspicious of my motives and my sanity; I just called him 'the youngest one' (Gen 44:2). Once they had left for home the next morning, I sent the steward after my brothers to accuse them of stealing my special cup. Naturally, they protested their innocence, fearing that their suspicions were valid that this wining and dining with the chief minister really was too good to be true. They insisted that none of them had stolen a thing and became too confident for their own good.

They offered my steward a deal which they were sure would vindicate their innocence. 'If any one of your servants is found to have it, he will die; and the rest of us will become my lord's slaves' (Gen 44:9). I allowed myself a smile when he reported the story to me. If only my brothers could have foreseen the future when their seventeen-year-old brother had described his dreams to them: they would be happy one day to call themselves my 'servants', and they would address me as 'lord'. I don't think they would have taken time to plot against me; I think they would have killed me on the spot.

A search was agreed, supervised by my steward who found the cup in Benjamin's sack. The other brothers reacted instantly: 'At this they tore their clothes. Then they all loaded their donkeys and returned to the city' (Gen 44:13). This was a terrible blow for them. They had deliberately deceived my father with their story about an attack on me by wild animals, but here was a real tragedy for them. They were far more afraid of returning to Jacob than they were of the wrath of Egypt because he was the kind of dad who had managed to achieve that kind of hold on his sons, while others fail miserably to win any paternal respect at all.

My brothers did grovel, exactly as I'd planned. I was still in the house when they came in, and they threw themselves on the ground in front of me. I accused them angrily, pretending that it was my powers of divination which had revealed the truth to me. (This was an Egyptian practice I had studied, but I am increasingly unhappy about it, and I believe that the deeper we move into our native Hebrew faith, the more we shall find that such activities are completely incompatible with God's requirement of us.)

Judah was the spokesman, and he hid nothing. We had caught them red-handed, and he was willing to confess, 'God has uncovered your servants' guilt' (Gen 44:16). He offered my brothers to me as slaves, another amusing irony. I couldn't resist one further twist of the knife and insisted that I could not possibly enslave all of them, only Benjamin was needed. At least I was sparing his life. 'Only the man who was found to have the cup will become my slave,' I assured him. 'The rest of you, go back to your father in peace' (Gen 44:17). I was playing with them, and Judah pleaded with me on behalf of the aged father he never dreamed that we shared. 'We have an aged father, and there is a young son born to him in his old age. His brother is dead, and he is the only one of his mother's sons left, and his father loves him' (Gen 44:20). My brothers were offering me the truth they bitterly resented as their plea both for Benjamin's release and their freedom from Jacob's scathing tongue. Judah ploughed on desperately, recounting the saga of recent events in which I had played a vital part by forcing my brothers to bring Benjamin to Egypt, despite Jacob's stubborn reluctance. It was fascinating as well as emotionally gruelling to discover his perspective on the story. 'Your servant my father said to us, "You know that my wife bore me two sons. One of them went away from me, and I said, 'He has surely been torn to pieces.' And I have not seen him since. If you take this one from me too and harm comes to him, you will bring my grey head down to the grave in misery" ' (Gen 44:27–29).

Judah could not know the unbearable impact his words were making on me. Unwittingly he described to a son his father's lasting grief for him. He took responsibility for stealing the cup, but he confessed more guilt than he realised since his plight stemmed directly from my brothers' assault on my life all those years ago. He tried emotional pressure to wear me down but his appeal cut deeper than he imagined. Almost ruthlessly he returned to the dark truth that my father had lost a son whom they thought was dead, but I stood before them, unrecognised as a living denial of their assumption. For Jacob, Joseph was gone, and the loss of his second favourite son, Benjamin, would completely finish the old man for whom Judah was making an urgent plea. In his mind Judah appealed to an Egyptian high official who seemed to behave unlike any Egyptian he had met before, but he was also appealing as one man to another, hoping against hope to arouse my sympathy for his torment. I wanted to tell him that his plea was from one brother to another, and was almost ready to do that, but not quite. He pressed on, 'Now then, please let your servant remain here as my lord's slave in place of the boy, and let the boy return with his brothers. How can I go back to my father if the boy is not with me? No! Do not let me see the misery that would come upon my father' (Gen 44:33–34). Was this a scared son trying to pull a fast one on me to avoid his father's anger? Or, was it an incredible offer of sacrificial love, volunteering to replace his brother in slavery so that the brother and his father could enjoy freedom? Judah moved me deeply, and I resisted my own cynicism.

It was time to forgive my brothers, openly and freely. My resentment against them had burned for years, as had their hatred of me. We had all found it easy to justify how we felt, and we had wronged each other. Whenever I hit rock bottom, this bitterness festered away inside me, hardening into an aggressive defiance when I rose to power. I had my brothers just where I wanted them when they came to Egypt looking for food, and I was reluctant to let them off the hook. Since then, I had satisfied myself by playing a cruel game with those who were helpless before me. I had returned to them in full measure their compliment of contempt and humiliation, and I had carefully removed the dignity on which they had wanted to stand. Now I was ready to risk exposing my heart to them because I couldn't contain my feelings any longer. I was about to draw back the veil of my disguise.

I emptied the room, ordering stewards, domestic staff, political advisers, personal attendants and body guards to leave us. Only my brothers were left with me, and those outside were as alarmed as they were curious at this sudden seizure by a man known for his aloof dignity. We were alone in an incredible reunion. The noise we made travelled well beyond the walls of my dining room, but it all began with a stunned silence as I made my shattering announcement. 'I am Joseph! Is my father still living?... I am your brother Joseph, the one you sold into Egypt!' (Gen 45:3, 4). My brothers said nothing, terrified into silence by my words. Horror, shock, amazement, the numbness of obvious guilt, relief—they were all visible on my brothers' faces, and they were quiet. They saw that the tables were turned, and I had total power over them. They were the ones in a deep cistern, and it was up to me to pull them up or leave them in it.

Such meetings never run to plan. They stood around me; quiet, broken men, racked by a visible remorse, and I began to talk. In my emotional state I talked and talked, trying desperately to hide my bursting heart and longing to tell them the full story. I needed to speak words of forgiveness to them, but I was fumbling as men do when they are out of their depths emotionally. I talked, but I'm not sure how much they heard me. They were too dazed to take it all in, and their response was more visible than audible as the colour drained from their faces. Each brother knew I could gloat over him if I so wished, but I didn't seem to be intent on destroying any of them. They allowed me to say as much as I wanted, deferring in fear and disbelief to the authority I was not yet willing to concede.

I can't remember all I said, which is probably a good thing. Those are not the kind of occasions you would choose to account for every word you've spoken. Words did tumble out, expressing and hiding much of what I wanted to say. I gave my brothers the gist of my life since they had abandoned me, assuring them of my commitment to an overruling plan of God which had slowly unfolded in my life. I pleaded with them to fetch my father to join the reunion party. 'Now hurry back to my father and say to him, "This is what your son Joseph says: God has made me lord of all Egypt. Come down to me; don't delay" Tell my father about all the honour accorded me in Egypt and about everything you have seen. And bring my father down here quickly' (Gen 45:9, 13). This was one family reunion even you would have enjoyed—I do know what they're normally like. I baited them by offering the bribe of provisions for the entire family for the remaining five years which we expected of famine, but their part of the bargain was a complete move to Egypt. My brothers had bred pretty well, but the large group would be no more than a drop in the ocean for Egypt's national budget. 'You shall live in the region of Goshen and be near me—you, your children and grandchildren, your flocks and herds, and all you have.' I knew I was tempting them, and I went on, 'I will provide for you there, because five years of famine are still to come. Otherwise you and your household and all who belong to you will become destitute' (Gen 45:10–11).

Eventually I stopped talking, but I had at least given them vital time to collect their thoughts. Our emotions broke loose in one of those moments most men fear but badly need. None of us held back, and we washed away the years of bitterness with our tears. I threw my arms round Benjamin and Benjamin threw his arms around me, both of us sobbing our hearts out. Then I kissed my brothers and cried all over them. Afterwards, they talked with me, pouring out our guilt and excitement. Benjamin was the special brother as far as I was concerned, and we both thought we were dreaming, pinching ourselves for reality; I was alive, he was with me in Egypt and we were together. Our brothers looked on incredulously, allowing us an exclusive reunion, but impatient to share this demonstration of love now that we were reconciled.

Don't ask me how long we talked; just use your imagination. Twelve of us, each bursting with questions and answers, explanations and confessions; each one eager to give his version of events, and willing to take his share of the blame. These were moments of rare masculine honesty when we put our pride to one side. Every brother bit the dust, me included. We listed our mistakes, and we acknowledged attitudes we no longer defended. We recognised accusations we had wanted to withdraw, and we gave apologies which were long overdue. As they spoke with me, I saw again how badly I had provoked them by my ambitious arrogance. My presumption as a boy had sheltered cockily behind my dad's unfailing protection. My confidence as a teenager, which was the product of good looks, excellent prospects and parental indulgence, had been blind to the warning signs my brothers posted. I had selfishly accepted every favour with an air of triumph over my brothers who were repeatedly deprived of such favours, and they seethed with jealous anger. I saw again the coat none of us wanted, but which I had flaunted as a

sign of my father's special love for me. My brothers knew that they had served my father loyally for much longer than I had, but they saw now that a father does not apportion his heart in gratitude for services rendered. It is a more irrational process than that, and it's often selfishly and thoughtlessly motivated. I think my brothers realised that there was nothing I had done which could justify the drastic punishment they had meted out, and they did not hide that from me. We felt together that we were all victims of Jacob and the women he had taken as wives: Rachel, Leah, Bilhah and Zilpah. That could have drawn us together very early in our lives, but we were too young to be objective, and too selfish to prevent ourselves falling apart in a hostility that was both malicious and mutual.

The more I talked with my brothers, the more they saw the past in a new light. I was the son of Rachel and had always known they resented me, but I wanted them to accept me as their younger brother. Tragically, the more I felt their active dislike, the more defensive I became. Once you become defensive, you either go into your shell or you become aggressive to hide what you're feeling, and I became aggressive. That led me into deep trouble with brothers who were already infuriated by my father's bias against them because they weren't sons of Rachel. I made matters far worse by pressing home every advantage I could squeeze from my father's persistent preference for anyone and anything connected with Rachel, and so we created a vicious circle which mixed antagonism with retaliation.

But the scales were falling from our eyes as we found each other for the first time. We shared the pain of remorse, the amazement of reunion and the miracle of reconciliation. The real Joseph at last appeared to my brothers, and they ceased to be a gang of bullies to me. Our sudden enthusiasm for the new future we glimpsed was tinged with regret for a past we could not reclaim. We longed to relive our younger days with the experience of grown men, and we vowed to live differently now that we had a second chance. We wanted to teach our children better ways as we naively imagined that our new wisdom would cancel every parental folly, and we enjoyed the illusion.

I had suffered so much hurt that I needed more than one emotional meeting before I could completely forgive those who had wronged me. Forgiveness is a single act, a conscious and difficult deed, but it is also a lengthy struggle. It tears up weeds of resentment but fresh shoots are always ready to spring up from a mass of underground roots. The notion that one big pull is enough to uproot everything is doomed to disappointment, and I suffered considerable anguish as I struggled to get rid of my own bitterness. I had to isolate each new shoot, cutting it off or tearing it out until no more shoots appeared; only then had I truly forgiven.

This act of forgiveness is an offering of love to someone who has wronged you. I had piled up heaps of ammunition to use against my brothers, and for years my mind had rehearsed their trial. I never stopped to think that they were blissfully unaware of me and I was the only one suffering from my resentment. Once my brothers sold me for a quick profit, they forgot all about me, although I never forgot them. Potiphar's wife added to my grievances, and I blamed my brothers for her. This parade of grudges flooded my mind as I resisted forgiving them. I knew that as soon as I forgave them I would surrender all ammunition in a new beginning where I'd be hopelessly vulnerable because I couldn't make any further reference to what had gone before; I would wipe it out for ever when I forgave my brothers, and that was risky. But I was at the point where I wanted to forgive, and I wanted the freedom for myself as well as for my brothers which would come when I forgave them. The moment must not slip from my grasp to end years of mutual hatred and bitterness.

We came together in reconciliation not because we

were big men bringing a mutual offering of rich mercy but because each of us saw his own sins, his own grudges and the hurt he had inflicted on his brothers. I was deeply ashamed of my youthful stupidity, and gulped awkwardly when I looked at it in a fresh light. My brothers, for their part, froze in horror when they met me as a human being and not as the monstrously spoiled brat for whom they felt neither affection nor concern. Our remorse made us ready to forgive, and to be forgiven.

We shared a moving reunion, and that was wonderful as far as it went. Now the hard part began. We had to make reconciliation practical in a new relationship where we could rediscover the original purpose for family life. Others had contributed to our troubles, and we extended to them the forgiveness we were sharing, releasing them in the freedom of merciful love, although as absent friends they knew nothing of what we were doing. The mood was infectious, and the Egyptians caught our joy. 'When the news reached Pharaoh's palace that Joseph's brothers had come, Pharaoh and all his officials were pleased' (Gen 45:16). Pharaoh couldn't wait to talk with me in person and was really generous in his response to our news. 'Tell your brothers, "Do this: load your animals and return to the land of Canaan, and bring your father and your families back to me. I will give you the best of the land of Egypt and you can enjoy the fat of the land" ' (Gen 45:17–18).

Pharaoh's welcome gesture to our family offered me an unexpected opportunity which I didn't hesitate to accept. I charged my brothers to return to Canaan to fetch my father, adding Pharaoh's authority to my previous instructions that the family should all come to Egypt to find temporary relief from the famine. Secretly, I hoped they would become permanent immigrants.

I had forgiven them; they had forgiven me, and the whole experience had been painful as well as a wonderful joy to us all. We did not solve every problem overnight because that is not what forgiveness does. We still had to live as twelve brothers, working each day at a new relationship which was bound to stretch our patience and our humour. But we had wiped away the past so that it no longer had the power to destroy us. The difficulties we faced now were only those of today and tomorrow, not those of yesterday which had lost the cancer of its bitterness. Slyly, as if testing the waters, I slipped in a teasing caution before they left for Canaan: 'Don't quarrel on the way' (Gen 45:24). I don't think they even heard me as they rushed off to bring my father to me. Day by day, God's overruling purpose for my life was becoming clearer, and I felt cleaner than I had been for years. Reconciliation with my brothers had lifted a great weight, and I had helped to shake it off.

All I had to do now was to wait with a fretting impatience for my father to arrive in Egypt. I wondered if his heart would take the strain. While I whiled away the time, thinking of nothing else and totally unable to concentrate on my work, I tried to imagine the scene at home when my brothers poured in with their amazing news. I chuckled noisily, happy to make public my private amusement.

9

My Father—Jacob

When you're very young your father can do no wrong. As you grow up he can do no right. In your teens he may appear to be the biggest fool under the sun; but within a few years you are pleasantly surprised by all that he has learned so quickly. These observations say little about your father, but they do offer a revealing commentary on your uncertain progress to maturity. You are taking time to come to terms with the natural frailty of an ordinary mortal who finds himself saddled with the dubious privilege of being the source of your entry into the world.

I took a long time to understand my father, Jacob, realising only gradually that the question in any issue of whether he was right or wrong was not relevant to the quality of our relationship. As a maturing adult, I made my own judgements about his wisdom or folly, but the real challenge for me was to understand him. Looking back, I still believe that Dad made some bad mistakes in the way he met the challenge of fatherhood. Why did he behave in such a partial and irrational way towards his sons? What provoked his irritable outbursts? Why didn't he do more when his wives were obviously so unhappy together? I was baffled for so long, but the difference now is that the passing years have brought me a much better understanding of how Dad felt in himself. Of course, he carries a heavy responsibility for his own actions, but I can see now that he's not the only one who needs someone loving enough to be alongside him in compassionate sympathy. We all need others who accept us, warts and all.

It is not difficult to condemn Jacob. He made glaring mistakes which have proved costly to many others besides himself. But I am a son describing his father. I'm speaking about the man who gave me life and it's painful for me to make public our family blunders. Jacob loved me: blindly, foolishly, even angrily, but he made no secret of what I meant to him. I suffered from his love, but I also benefited from it. Above all, I have seen how the purpose of God transformed his short-sighted stupidity so that he made an enormous contribution to our lives as brothers. The more that sons and daughters allow you into their confidence the more you see how many men find parenthood difficult despite the best of intentions, and you despair of the damage which fathers inflict on their children, wittingly or unwittingly. At least my father never had malicious intentions against any of us, and we certainly suffered no physical abuse from him. But few of us who are fathers can afford to be complacent about our performance, or blind to our own shortcomings. There are a few things I've done or failed to do as a dad which I'd give a lot to be able to change.

The most important thing a father can do for his child is to love that child's mother. Time and again, people have confided in me, trusting the leadership I exercised over them. Perhaps all leadership, even that which is purely political, has a pastoral dimension as people recognise an authority which has to be personally directive if it is to be truly effective. These confidences which I have been privileged to share have shown me that children do need the love of their parents; it would be ridiculous to suggest anything else. But there is a further security which children crave, and that is the security of the relationship between Mum and Dad. In loving the mother of his children, the father is saying something vital to them, and their behaviour will be badly affected when hostility, apathy or even betrayal blot out that love. We need to offer very practical support to families who find themselves divided at this point of critical need.

When he faced the challenge of loving the mother of his children, my father both succeeded and failed. I always knew how much he loved Rachel, pouring himself out to her as much in her death as in her life. Benjamin and I grew up in the total assurance that our father loved our mother, and nothing could destroy the foundation which this gave our lives. Benjamin had lost his mother at his birth (Gen 35:16–18), but he was greatly comforted later by his discovery of the love which had burned between his parents. But our brothers were deprived of this confidence. They had different mothers from Benjamin and me. We were sons of Rachel, but they were sons of Rachel's older sister, Leah, and of the respective servants of Rachel and Leah, Bilhah and Zilpah (Gen 35:22–26). They deeply resented our father's unconcealed preference for Rachel, and they never really forgave him for the disadvantages they suffered from the lesser love he offered to the three women who were their mothers. Strangely, Jacob proved in most other ways a marvellous father to them, which they were quite willing to admit. Each brother was disturbed by the paternal discrepancy which prevented the harmony we might otherwise have enjoyed as one big family. My father withheld from my brothers the greatest gift he could have given them, and we all paid a heavy price. You can't be too surprised that my brothers had no scruples about deceiving their father that I was dead (Gen 37:31–35). Two aspects of retribution came together at this point to plunge Jacob into lasting mourning for me and also for himself.

First, the chickens of deceit came home to roost. It was ironic that he who had actively deceived his brother Esau, and his father Isaac, with the initiative of his mother Rebekah, now found himself forced to take a dose of his own medicine. This was reflected in Jacob's obvious bitterness when my brothers returned from Egypt seeking permission to take Benjamin back to meet the demand of a stranger who was responsible for the food distribution in that terrible famine. 'Their father Jacob said to them, "You have deprived me of my children. Joseph is no more and Simeon is no more, and now you want to take Benjamin. Everything is against me!...My son will not go down there with you; his brother is dead and he is the only one left" ' (Gen 42:36, 38). My father spoke only of Benjamin and me in that outburst, dismissing our other brothers as less than sons because Rachel was not their mother; and that really was asking for trouble. He gave further vent to his feelings when he saw that he had no choice but to release Benjamin to travel back to Egypt with my brothers. 'As for me, if I am bereaved, I am bereaved,' he cried (Gen 43:14).

Secondly, the consequences of a biased love came home to my father. Jacob had treated two sons with such favour that the other ten were bound to be disgruntled, and they were! When he agreed that Benjamin should return to Egypt, my father spoke of him by name, 'And may God Almighty grant you mercy before the man so that he will let...Benjamin come back with you' (Gen 43:14). By contrast, he referred to Simeon not by name but as 'your other brother' (Gen 43:13). I'm sure Jacob meant nothing by this, but that's not how it sounded to his sons and they strongly resented what they heard because it was the kind of lapse which Dad repeated too often for it to be a coincidence. Benjamin and I were never anonymous, but other brothers frequently were.

My father's love was unfortunate for all concerned. His unhealthy regard for two favourite sons produced unreasonable attitudes in me which did me no service. I expected attention from those who had no reason to subscribe to my dad's view of me, in fact they probably had good reason to disagree violently with him. He, for his part, failed to put a stop to my selfish outbursts at home and I found it hard to understand why he was so angered by my dreams (Gen 37:10). He never prepared me for the rough and tumble of wider community life, and the corners my brothers plotted to knock off were removed too brutally to achieve the desired effect.

In his defence, my father's love was not entirely negative, but he spoilt it by his selfish blindness to the effect he was having on us as twelve brothers, not as two brothers and ten hangers-on. By contrast, he gave me a wonderful sense of my own value, and I knew that he loved me. Nothing he ever said or did caused me to doubt that. It never occurred to me then to wish that my brothers had shared this priceless gift so that we could all have enjoyed my father's regard, but that's what I wish now. The power he held over us was that of emotional influence not of physical force, and he misused it as far as my brothers were concerned.

I believe that my father's own upbringing had moulded him too rigidly. He grew up in an environment of deceit, and he quickly learned how to play his part in the intrigue which was by now a family pastime. My grandmother Rebekah, was always ready to do anything to secure maximum advantage for her cause and she encouraged Jacob in his deceit. Rachel followed her mother-in-law in securing a strong hold over Jacob. She knew the problems of child-bearing were hers and not his, but she blamed him before he could come up with an alternative explanation. 'When Rachel saw that she was not bearing Jacob any children, she became jealous of her sister. So she said to Jacob, "Give me children, or I'll die" ' (Gen 30:1). He ought to have retorted immediately that he had already proved himself perfectly capable of fathering children, so what was wrong with her? But Rachel was too strong and

Jacob too weak for him to make the point strike home. On one occasion Rachel did go too far and Jacob bit back at her, 'Jacob became angry with her and said, "Am I in the place of God, who has kept you from having children?" ' (Gen 30:2), but that was a rare exception. Rachel was quite happy to offer her servant Bilhah, provided she could wrest the initiative away from her older sister Leah. 'Then Rachel said, "I have had a great struggle with my sister, and I have won" ' (Gen 30:8).

My father knew what I meant to Rachel, and when she died giving birth to Benjamin he tried to make up to me what I had lost in her death. He should have known that no father can be a mother without ceasing to be a father. Jacob took something away from me when he was trying to give me more, and I took years to overcome the hindrance of his generous favour which was blinded by bereavement and age.

It can't be easy to be a wise father to twelve sons, to say nothing of a few daughters (Gen 30:21; 34:1; 46:7). It is even harder when these children are the products of four different mothers. My dad's big mistake was that he failed to spot the problem, which made it impossible for him to respond to its challenge. It could all have been great fun and a big laugh, but it wasn't. My reluctant conclusion now, however lovingly I try to soften the blow, is that we were all victims of one man's inherited selfishness.

I believe Jacob was selfish in taking four women to be his wives. I accept that this was perfectly reasonable in our culture, but his motives were entirely selfish. He must have known about the chaotic unrest among the women he brought into motherhood, but once he had the sons he wanted from Rachel he didn't seem to care about any other upheavals in the home. If only he had thought more carefully from the beginning. It's all very well to say that something is culturally acceptable, but that doesn't make it morally right. We can laugh about it or take the matter seriously, but either way, one woman is enough for any man. Jacob took more wives because he wanted children how and when he wanted them. He used four women as a means to his own ends, and that's selfish in my book. Any objective onlooker could have warned him of the inevitable outcome, but Jacob never listened to counsel he didn't like. He knew what he wanted, and he lived in a society which placed few restrictions on the freedom of a husband to do things his own way. The women were there for his convenience, and that was how he treated them, with neither patience nor regard for their unhappy squabbles.

Jacob poured his love into me, but he was indulging his fatherly pride and pleasure. A thin line separates the selfishness of parents from natural pride in their own children. The desire Jacob felt to be generous to me was mixed with a proud spirit which wanted public affirmation of his son. I was used to satisfy a father who had waited too long to be satisfied.

When I became the hapless victim of violence, Jacob grieved for himself. He spent little time in distress at the way he thought I'd been torn to pieces, but he demanded constant attention for his suffering as a bereaved father. He oozed self-pity, and my brothers saw through his endless repetition of tragic loss. Joseph may have lost his life, but Jacob had lost a son, which he clearly felt was far worse (Gen 42:36).

I'll never know how Jacob could be so absorbed in himself that he failed to deal with the dreadful relationships between those of us who found ourselves thrown together as half-brothers. Men and women were jostling for his attention and he accepted the struggle with no apparent concern for our distress. There was so much he could have done, but he did so little. His blissful ignorance of all this aggravated the wound for my brothers and stirred their malice against me. I reacted defensively but arrogantly, and you know the rest of the story. One man's selfishness wreaked havoc among his sons. Benjamin and

I seemed to fare best of all, but I eventually paid a heavy price, and it did Benjamin no good to be as pampered as he was. His brothers' tolerance was not matched in the wider community of Canaan and Egypt.

When Jacob heard of corn in Egypt, he sent his sons to investigate. But things did not turn out as he wished, and he soon faced a threat to the life of Benjamin, or that's how he saw it. You could sum up my father's total reaction in a few words, 'How will this affect me?' As if the rest of us were unaffected! Simeon could well have lost his life, and he did suffer a temporary loss of freedom which he accepted willingly in love for his father. Benjamin himself might have been killed or lost for ever as a slave in Egypt. Reuben was ready to sacrifice two sons for the peace of mind of a father whose sole concern was himself. You probably think I'm hard on my dad, but I just wish he had been less self-centred in his example to us. Isaac and Rebekah have a lot to answer for in the way they must have brought him up!

We all use our upbringing to defend ourselves. Every counsellor goes back to the childhood of those who seek his help, trying to find the source of continuing problems, but there must come a time when we accept full responsibility for our lives even if we still need help. I'm not laying down any particular stage of life, but I don't see how you can delay it beyond parenthood. If you are responsible for children who depend on you for protection, example, guidance, friendship and fun, you can't go on sheltering in the failings of your parents as an excuse for your own needs. Jacob had his excuses. His elders were anything but wise with him, but his sons looked to him for something better than they received. However much I love him, I don't agree that we can pass the buck back to Isaac and Rebekah, who in turn will pass it back to Abraham and Sarah. The buck stops with Jacob.

I do feel disloyal, almost treacherous in spelling out my view of the truth, but I'm doing no more than echoing your probable judgements on a man called Jacob who also happened to be my father. Frankly, our family life was a fiasco, with my father at the heart of the trouble. My reflections have not endeared him to me, but I understand him far better now and I feel able to be much more merciful than he might reasonably expect of me. You do reach the stage, at least as an adult, where you see your father's faults, you recognise the serious problems he created, but you owe him something you can never repay. It's tied up with the gift of life which has forged a unique bond between you, and it is the reason why honesty compels me to paint a picture which is less than flattering, but also to confess that I loved this man. A genuine paradox lays facts side by side which are really in tension, but are also accurate expressions of the truth. I declare a paradox in my assessment of my father. In understanding him, I forgive his failings and I appreciate his awful sense of loss when I disappeared and Benjamin came under threat. In describing him I must tell you how many people were victims of a selfish man. I do think there were signs of remorse, almost imperceptible, but signs nonetheless. Jacob realised his mistakes, although he found it as difficult to admit them as most fathers do.

I see my father in his older years—hurt, bewildered and yet proud. He smelt something fishy about my alleged death, but he was not shrewd enough to suspect my brothers. He puzzled over the circumstances whose blessing had suddenly deserted him, and his powers of cunning lost their usual ability to bring him out on top. He had taken for granted the material favour of his God, the God of his fathers, Abraham and Isaac, but now he had to enquire more closely into the nature of One whose character had not recently concerned him. In his younger, keener days, my father had struggled almost physically to know God, and to experience his awesome presence. The holiness of God had overwhelmed him in his dream. 'When Jacob awoke from his sleep, he thought, "Surely the Lord is in this place, and I was not aware of it." He was afraid and said, "How awesome is this place! This is none other than the house of God; this is the gate of heaven" ' (Gen 28:16–17). He had pleaded with God to accompany his expedition to find a wife, knowing how vital it was to live under the sun of his blessing, and he had been quite specific as he set out. 'If God will be with me and will watch over me on this journey I am taking and will give me food to eat and clothes to wear so that I return safely to my father's house, then the Lord will be my God. This stone that I have set up as a pillar will be God's house, and of all that you give me I will give you a tenth' (Gen 28:20–22). But that godly desire weakened with time, and Dad became unwilling to be tested by awkward circumstances. Despite his sadness, he always believed himself to be a Patriarch, a creator of something more than his own family, and he expected due deference from his sons and wives. Cantankerous to the end, he defied a desperate Reuben with his insistence, 'My son will not go down there with you; his brother is dead and he is the only one left' (Gen 42:37). The old man was difficult, stubbornly difficult, but I saw into his heart when I thought about his life, and I found something breaking and broken. Once you discover a broken heart, you find a new capacity to be merciful to an unspoken plea for understanding.

Jacob was waiting in Canaan for my brothers to return with corn and with Benjamin. He was afraid, tense and hungry, and the days passed slowly, teasing the limited resources of his patience. He had no idea when his sons would be back nor did he suspect that they were on their way as errand boys for Pharaoh. So far from losing his life, Benjamin had received the best treatment of all. 'Pharaoh...gave them provisions for their journey. To each of them he gave new clothing, but to Benjamin he gave three hundred shekels of silver and five sets of clothes' (Gen 45:21–22). With customary respect for age, Pharaoh had added special gifts for Jacob—'ten donkeys loaded with the best things of Egypt, and ten female donkeys loaded with corn and bread and other provisions for his journey' (Gen 45:23). The gifts were apparently from me, but Pharaoh had authorised them. I gave them the carts which Pharaoh had commanded (Gen 45:26), and Jacob had a surprise coming to him.

Jacob was looking out; he did nothing else all day once he judged their return to be imminent. Day after day he waited for sons he considered to be overdue, pacing as restlessly as an anxious husband fretting over a wife in her first labour. With his quiver full of offspring, my father of all people should have learned how to wait in peace. The retinue finally came into view as a dot on the horizon which slowly grew larger. As it drew nearer to home, my brothers jumped off in a spontaneous and undignified race to be first with the news. The result was a dead heat and an unrehearsed chorus: 'Joseph is still alive! In fact, he is ruler of all Egypt' (Gen 45:26).

You can long for something to happen, you can ache for its fulfilment, you can plunge from the heights of optimism to the depths of despair and back again, but when your dream comes true you refuse to believe the news. 'Jacob was stunned; he did not believe them' (Gen 45:26). Perhaps the chickens of deception really were coming home to roost and Jacob was afraid of bad news from sons whose track record offered no grounds for confidence. Only when they produced the gifts I'd arranged for them did my father agree that he had unmistakable evidence from them. 'I'm convinced! My son Joseph is still alive. I will go and see him before I die' (Gen 45:28).

The return to Egypt took the family via Beersheba where Dad insisted on a break. He was an old man and no longer travelled with ease, but all older people need regular stops on long journeys and my brothers were expecting some delays. But it was more than that with Beersheba. The local shrine was an ideal place for Dad to give honour to God whose welcome intervention he acknowledged

(Gen 46:1). In his private worship, Jacob saw God and heard him speak. His physical eyes and ears detected nothing, but his spiritual faculties were alert to the One who approached him. He told me later of an impression almost visual, and of words almost audible, which came to him as long as his eyes were shut. He found it easier to move away from natural scenes when his eyes were shut, and God led him into a magnificent view of spiritual reality. A voice called his name, as if unaware that he was already seeking God. ' "Jacob! Jacob!" "Here I am," he replied' (Gen 46:2). My father's body was failing him, but his spirit knew no such weakness, and his response was immediate: 'Here I am.' That's a dangerous thing to say if you have no idea what is coming next—a summons, a rebuke, a promise, or even a complete change in your life; it could be anything. This time, it was a mighty reassurance which encouraged my father to continue his eager journey without fear: 'I am God, the God of your father. Do not be afraid to go down to Egypt, for I will make you into a great nation there' (Gen 46:3).

These are the early days of our Hebrew faith, but I foresee that the word of God will often challenge our fear. He will not allow us to shelter behind feelings which cower before threatening danger. He will make demands on us which sometimes seem unreasonable, even impossible but also wonderful, to take a firm grip on ourselves and to move ahead in trust. 'Do not be afraid' will become a motto of Hebrew faith, a stirring summons to personal religion and corporate action, as well as a valid hunting ground for hungry preachers (eg, see Genesis 26:24; Deuteronomy 1:21; 20:1; Joshua 1:9; Isaiah 44:8; Jeremiah 1:8).

Their journey to Egypt proceeded with the transport Pharaoh had provided. 'Jacob left Beersheba, and Israel's sons took their father Jacob and their children and their wives in the carts that Pharaoh had sent to transport him' (Gen 46:5). It was a large group, incredibly well stocked for such deprived times, as it wended its way towards the land of food, welcome and reunion. 'All those who went to Egypt with Jacob—those who were his direct descendants, not counting his son's wives—numbered sixty-six persons' (Gen 46:26). I met them at Goshen after my father, typically, had sent Judah ahead to Egypt to ask me for precise directions. I think he still feared a trick.

It's difficult to describe my reunion with my father. It was one of those moments a man regards as too private to discuss, although he knows many saw what happened. We said very little; both of us were far too overcome for words as the years of heartache spilled over into tears (Gen 46:29). Words fail us in our deepest times, discarded because they trivialise what is taking place. My father had scarcely dared to live for such a day as this, dreaming without any realistic expectation of its dawning. 'Now I am ready to die,' he said, 'since I have seen for myself that you are still alive' (Gen 46:30).

I advised my family that they would do well to describe themselves at all times as life-long shepherds who had the care of livestock in their blood. In that way they would be left free to settle in Goshen, a particularly fertile region. The Egyptians have a strange contempt for shepherds but would not create unhelpful pressure for my family if they stayed in Goshen. I promised to pave the way by speaking to Pharaoh before he met them, which he was keen to do (Gen 46:31, 34). The idea worked well, and Pharaoh responded predictably when he said to me, 'Your father and your brothers have come to you and the land of Egypt is before you; settle your father and your brothers in the best part of the land. Let them live in Goshen' (Gen 47:5–6). He was anxious to meet my father who used his greater age skilfully to overcome Pharaoh's superior position. 'Jacob blessed Pharaoh and went out from his presence' (Gen 47:7, 10). Pharaoh was not accustomed to being blessed; he did the blessings, and he sentenced those who were not blessed. My father had turned the tables on him, and I enjoyed the family gift for crafty advantage.

Dad settled into his home with remarkable flexibility. He was artful by nature, and a large family had forced him to be flexible in attitude which he retained to a surprising degree in his old age. He lived a further seventeen years in Egypt, pleading only that when he died, we would return him to the resting place of our forefathers, a perfectly reasonable request which we expected Pharaoh to grant willingly. When he sensed that he was going to die soon, my father called for me and said, 'If I have found favour in your eyes, put your hand under my thigh and promise that you will show me kindness and faithfulness. Do not bury me in Egypt, but when I rest with my fathers, carry me out of Egypt and bury me where they are buried' (Gen 47:29–30). Jacob's eyesight grew steadily worse until he was almost blind, which sparked off further emotional incidents. He wanted to see my two sons Manasseh and Ephraim, so I brought them close to him for him to hug them and kiss them. His voice was breaking as he whispered to me, 'I never expected to see your face again, and now God has allowed me to see your children too' (Gen 48:10–11). He was deeply moved and so was I, but I was also a bit embarrassed as often happens when elderly parents become unusually emotional.

We were watching our father's mental and physical deterioration which is always painful for relatives who can remember much fitter days. He began to repeat himself, demanding to bless everyone he could lay his hands on. He blessed my sons, insisting on the alarming reversal of the firstborn and the secondborn (Gen 48:20). Perhaps this was his own justification of the deception he had practised on his brother Esau. I protested vigorously, but there was no stopping my father once he was in full swing. He blessed whom he blessed, and that was that. He blessed his own sons, each one of us in turn, with some bruising comments thrown in with the blessings (Gen 49:1–28). He concluded all this with specific instructions for his burial and, satisfied at last, he died (Gen 49:33).

In our culture the customary mourning period is lengthy and complicated, but in Egypt it was more so than usual, extending over seventy days and including extravagant embalming. That time helped us to grieve naturally; nothing was bottled up and we found personal healing in our bereavement. I've no idea how you cope if you live in a country which suppresses emotion as an unnecessary sign of weakness. I grieved freely, and I found strength to carry on living; I didn't fall apart.

Jacob was no saint; he was a weak, fallible and crafty man who used other people for his own ends, and many suffered in the process. But his heart also beat with love, and in his clumsy attempt at fatherhood he wanted the best for me even if he failed the sons who didn't have Rachel for a mother. We weren't suffering from Jacob's cruelty but from his selfish stupidity. You have read the story for yourself, and I shall not repeat it, old man as I am. I ask you to respect my honesty. I have not painted my father in glowing colours, and I accept suggestions which have been made to me that much of Jacob is likely to reappear in his own sons, me included. I have tried to overcome the difficulties which that has caused for my family and the vast circle with whom I come into contact. Where I have failed, I will not try to blame my father; he shoulders enough resonsibility as it is. For me, Jacob has one vital, redeeming feature; he was my father, and for me that makes him unique among men. The blessing he gave me was not the blessing of his final words, but of the total assurance of his love in which I always lived. I loved him, unashamedly, in return.

10

The Guidance of God—a Testimony

The course of my life has taken me to the heights and plunged me to the depths, causing me to live precariously in favour and to fall disastrously from it. This has made me wonder if there has been any reason behind it all. Or has it been no more than a matter of chance dealt to me by a very indifferent hand?

Who has been pulling the strings of my life all these years? Was it my father Jacob? However you look at it, you have to conclude that he exercised an enormous influence over my destiny. It was beneficial in terms of the security I gained from my assurance of his unwavering love, but destructive in terms of the suffering which resulted from his provocation of my brothers who turned on me. (I've already admitted several times that I provoked them as well!) In my opinion, my father has been the key person in my development.

But what about Pharaoh? He gave me power. Had it not been for him, I would not have risen to the position of authority which I occupy in Egypt, and I can't think of any other way in which our family reunion would have been achieved. Pharaoh brought my own dreams to fulfilment, changing the course of my family's future and possibly that of the entire Hebrew people who will always remember Egypt when they declare their essential faith (eg, see Exodus 13:8–9; 16:6; 1 Chronicles 17:21; Psalm 114:1; Hosea 11:1; 12:13).

Do I hear a protest from Potiphar's wife? Yes, she too had a tremendous influence on the course of events, if not on me personally. She thrust me into the place, admittedly an Egyptian prison, where I became available to Pharaoh and to power. Her intentions against me were totally negative, but she also moved me at just the right time.

This question 'who was pulling the strings?' becomes more complicated. We can't leave my brothers out of the picture. They rejected me from home and eventually sold me into slavery. They initiated the move which took me to Egypt, and they arrived on my doorstep years later to prompt our amazing reconciliation. Perhaps my brothers would claim that they pulled the vital strings and I was a puppet in their determined hands. Presumably we should include my mother Rachel, the prison officer in Egypt who promoted me, and the cup-bearer who finally remembered to mention me to Pharaoh. They all deserve a place in this roll of dubious honour.

But don't forget me. It may seem to you that I was always the victim of chance circumstances. My brothers moved me around, as did Potiphar's wife, Potiphar himself, and Pharaoh, but I refuse to let anyone dismiss me as the passive spectator of my own life. I responded quickly to every opportunity which came my way. I saw genuine possibilities for advancement, and I seized them all. I never held back when I knew I had a contribution to make, whether serving well in Potiphar's domestic routine, offering to explain dreams in Egypt, or running the country for a desperate Pharaoh.

So who was pulling the strings? Is there a meaning to my life, or do we write it off as a series of random events which conspired through serious setbacks to end happily ever after? Perhaps we should speak of an impersonal force of fate which has moved relentlessly through the years, paying no heed to the human puppets who dangle on the end of its strings, but I find that conclusion to be one of despair which is also an unconvincing explanation of the full facts.

Let me tell you what I think. You don't have to agree with me, but at least give me a fair hearing. I have suffered bitter betrayal from a number of people I trusted. My brothers, Potiphar's wife, and the forgetful butler all did the dirty on me, and I sank more than once from highest favour to extreme humiliation. That certainly raises some important religious questions which I don't intend to ignore. But my main response at the end of my life is one of great thankfulness. God has been at work all my life, and I don't see that as a matter of strings being pulled. The fact that I couldn't see how he was at work for so long doesn't prevent me from seeing it now as I look back. It is in looking back that I realise how inappropriate it is to speak of God pulling the strings. He has intertwined his will with my response to produce a story which is utterly personal. He has been the vital power in my life, but he's done that mysteriously through the complex human relationships which have lifted me up and thrown me down.

I have planned for a long time to write my story because I want to tell you about a truth which explains it all. I have lived through a puzzle which has fitted together very slowly, piece by piece, but only God has known the complete picture. He allowed me one clue which was my dreams, and they strengthened me in my darkest days. Now I am a very old man, and I don't have much time left. My plea is that you don't stop with the thrilling details of my adventures but that you search for the key to their meaning, as I have searched. This will unlock so much of your own life to you.

God has held the key all the time, even when I was sure he'd thrown it away or lost it. I grew up believing that he was with me, and although that faith faltered badly on

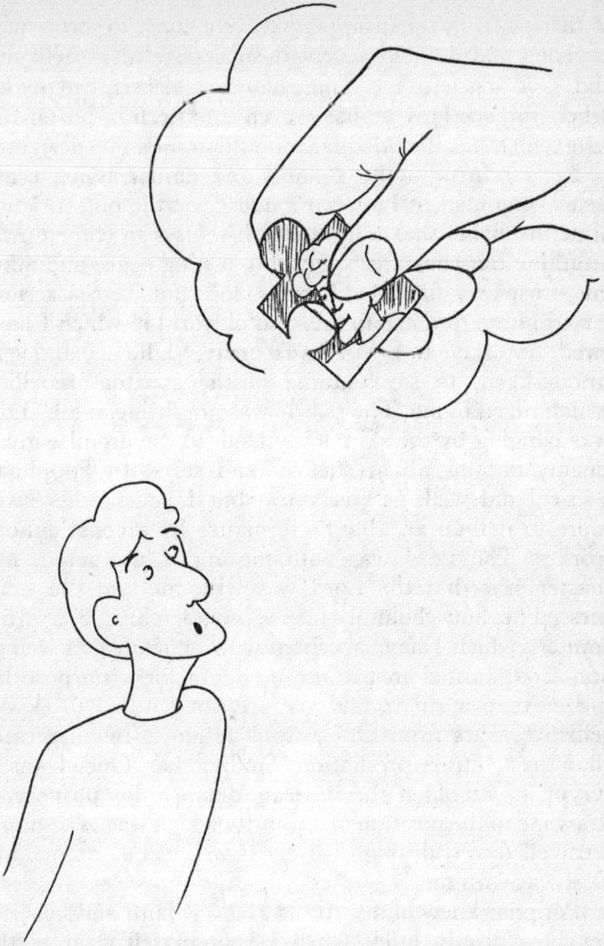

occasions, it never disappeared. I've come to terms with disaster and I have accepted success, always believing that God was with me. You will only make sense of my life when you see how he has woven a pattern of purposeful love which has included far more than me in its design.

Let's return to the squalid and embarrassing scene which unfolded in Potiphar's house. At the outset, I will state my belief that a faith which refuses to contemplate anything but constant protection, lasting peace and affluent prosperity for its adherents does not have a serious contribution to make to the kind of world in which I have lived. As a slave in Egypt I was lonely, frightened and very discouraged, to say nothing of the spiritual rebellion which raged in me. The puzzle was not fitting at all, and I was clinging by the skin of my teeth to the promise given by my dreams about sheaves and stars. In Potiphar's house I did well, as you know, but I believe there was more to it than an able performance by a conscientious worker. The Lord was with me and I prospered. My master saw that the Lord was with me and the Lord blessed his household because of me (Gen 39:2, 3, 5). In a mystery which I have accepted with reluctance as well as joy, God wanted to use me in Egypt for a purpose far bigger than a single life. We are not entitled to expect selfish favours from One whose design is much greater than the arbitrary promotion of individuals. Once I was in Egypt, he unfolded the intricate detail of his purpose to draw me to the position of authority which was to be mine. I travelled to it through valleys as well as mountains, but God was with me.

Potiphar knew of my strong Hebrew faith and he spotted how deeply I felt when I kept myself clear of the Egyptian practices which would have compromised it. He respected me, accepting my convictions about the blessing of God to both of us. He had no difficulty with the Egyptian gods blessing Egyptians and the Hebrew God blessing Hebrews, happily allowing me to acknowledge only one God if I didn't mind depriving myself of the enjoyment he gained from an impotent variety of metal deities. He refused to agree with me, but he was still amused when I teased him that his fortunes had improved considerably since I entered his service with the faith of a Hebrew (Gen 39:5). Potiphar thanked his gods and I praised the Lord for the same blessings in the same house. I think my belief impressed him, that all life, all the time, in every sphere, comes under the careful eye of God. I argued that it's not enough to sacrifice to God one day of the week, or one time of each day, if we live selfishly the rest of the time. That was partly why I refused the advances of Potiphar's wife, whatever the cost of denying her. I refused her, but I honoured God (Gen 39:9–10).

The situation was almost the same when Potiphar had me thrown into prison. I was suffering punishment for an offence I did not commit, and that provoked again the questions which had arisen when my brothers dumped me in the cistern: where is God now? Why has he allowed this to happen? Is this the end of my life? But the purpose of God to direct me his way and to use me, even in a prison where he had so few witnesses, continued to weave its intricate pattern. While I was there, the Lord was with me, showing me kindness and favour as the prison warder took notice of me. Whatever I tried, it seemed to work well (Gen 39:20–23). I struggled to rid myself of bitterness, so that I could speak of God and my confidence in him. I received abusive mockery which dismissed me with scorn, but there were also listening ears among the prisoners who wondered how a man could languish in prison but confess God was with him.

Although I suffered betrayal and imprisonment, you may be tempted to remind me that I did do rather well in Potiphar's house and in the Egyptian jail. The problem that creates for me is that any reflection on the loving purpose of God can sound like a smug contemplation of success with little to offer those who do not rise to power as

I did. I can only ask you to catch the heart of what I'm trying to communicate—God is at work in every aspect of our lives. I was often quite unable to answer my own questions, so I'm not likely to make much headway with yours. If God was blessing me, was he cursing those who did not share my blessing? Was he with me because he had deserted the others? If he was with me, why did I become the victim of gross injustice and vindictive assault? Or do my questions come from a completely inadequate view of God himself? I have to accept the force of these questions, but I can't answer them convincingly, at least not in the way they have been put.

We must look at your life from your perspective, and at my life from mine, so that we allow God maximum freedom to deal differently with us. We can't retreat into a selfish preoccupation with each individual, but we need to remember that he has always taken a personal interest in us which has included his call for us to respond fully to him. I'm not saying that God was with me when things went well but he deserted me in the tough times. My testimony is that I have known his presence in the heights and the depths, and I have not hidden from the bitterness of my own plight. God's pleasure does not carry a guarantee of automatic success, and difficulty does not indicate his obvious anger. I can't prove to you that the Lord was with me in Potiphar's house, certainly not if you want to be cynical, but I can tell you what I felt at the time, how it affected my understanding of the strange progress of events, and how it all seems to me now.

Guidance and the past

It is a widely held view that God's guidance is no more than a retrospective wisdom which tries to make sense of the past. We often urge young people to trust God but warn them that they will have no real assurance until they can look back and see that things have fitted together for them. My understanding of God has much more faith at its heart. It's a faith which is positive in the present and goes ahead with a stronger conviction for the future. That faith has been strengthened by my belief that the Lord has vindicated every commitment I made in the past to trust the way he chose for me, but it's been a real struggle to reach such a conclusion.

We need to make sense of life. We have to put the question 'why?' in all sorts of circumstances. Sometimes we are saying, 'I know there is a purpose of God in all this, and I want to find out what it is and embrace its lesson.' At other times we're saying, 'What have I done to deserve this suffering? Will someone please tell me why it's happened to me?' The first question looks up, and the second looks down, but both are asking 'why?' I asked 'why?' many times; when I was looking up and when I was looking down. The answers I found depended where I was looking at the time I put the question.

We followed the customary mourning rites when my father died. The entire family revolved around him, and he had revelled in the attention he received, not least in those last seventeen years in Egypt. Now he was gone, and a huge gap existed which would not be filled. Such is the passing of a father or mother that it's a waste of time trying to fill a gap which is not meant to be filled. I prefer to think of bereavement as a wound which will heal with time, leaving scars as the permanent sign that it has healed but it can't be forgotten. We followed our Hebrew mourning customs, and the Egyptians held their own funeral rites for my father in which I shared. The Canaanites looked on mystified as they watched the alien Egyptians and their own brother participating in rites they knew were foreign and suspected were unhelpful.

They sounded so profound as they commented on the obvious: 'The Egyptians are holding a solemn ceremony of mourning' (Gen 50:11). As if Egyptian mourning rites could be mistaken for a party! We gave Dad the burial for which he had pleaded, although I don't honestly see what difference it could make to him where he was buried. It puzzles me why so many people are concerned about where or how their funeral takes place, but it seems to be the thing to do, and I'm issuing my own instructions. Previous generations have tied me up with their requests, and I am returning the compliment to those who survive me, since it's too late to take revenge on my predecessors; but don't you think it's a bit stupid? What difference can it possibly make where they bury you or what they sing at the service. It's a sign either of our vanity or of our inadequate view of death, at least that's how it seems to me; and I was even more outspoken about it when I was younger. After we buried my father we trekked back to Egypt and life went on (Gen 50:14).

My brothers must have been afraid that my mood would change as soon as Dad was out of the way, as if he had been the only check on my conduct. They said among themselves, 'What if Joseph holds a grudge against us and pays us back for all the wrongs we did to him?' (Gen 50:15). To be honest, I thought our reunion had been completely genuine, and I was disappointed to be proved wrong. I appreciate that my authority in Egypt was a big threat to them, but I hoped I'd done enough to dispel their fears. I regarded our dispute as finished. In their fear, they tried to pull the wool over my eyes with a blatant arm-twister, and they nearly succeeded. They sent a message to me, 'Your father left these instructions before he died: I ask you to forgive your brothers the sins and the wrongs they committed in treating you so badly. Now please forgive the sins of the servants of the God of your father' (Gen 50:16–17). I don't know why I cried, but I think their evident mistrust of the forgiveness I had already extended to them, as well as their obvious fear of me, was too much when I was still upset about my father's death (Gen 50:17). I saw through their arm-twister, but I had no intention of harming any of them.

I suddenly realised how much I had pondered the past. For years I had struggled to find any meaning to my life, and my faith was often stretched to breaking point. How was God with me when Potiphar's wife betrayed me? What did it mean to claim that he was there all the time? I knew I was powerless, but I didn't expect to discover that God too was impotent, especially when I pleaded with him to show his hand. My brothers had not been through the same questioning agony as I had. Until recently, they had no reason to ask awkward questions for themselves or for Canaan, and they attributed the famine to nothing more than the disadvantage of life in a hot country. Now they were grovelling before me, as they had grovelled at our first meeting in Egypt. They threw themselves on the ground in front of me and spoke as one man, 'We are your slaves' (Gen 50:18).

I led my brothers into my view of God's guidance, 'Don't be afraid. Am I in the place of God? You intended to harm me, but God intended it for good to accomplish what is now being done, the saving of many lives' (Gen 50:19–20). I knew my theory was open to question, to objection and even to dismissal, but it was much more than a theory, it was my living testimony to God's power. If he wanted me in Egypt, if he wanted to save my family, if he is preparing us for a great future, if there is to be a dramatic exit from Egypt, can't he do it in a way that's painless and joyful? Yes, I've followed that path of reasoning, but it led me into a cul-de-sac. I trace the hand of God at work, a personal hand of love which has mapped out my way; not an easy way nor a welcome one, but a sure way. It has led me down into valleys and up on to mountains, but it has achieved its purpose. My brothers plotted to destroy me and they took action, but my dreams prepared me to survive their attacks and fulfil my destiny. God was at work also to bring me to power in Egypt, and the whole thing is so much clearer as I look back than ever it could have been at the time. If I had had no faith and no dreams, the disasters which hit me would have broken me. I was bewildered enough as it was! I can only be grateful that I've learnt to think my way through suffering as well as blessing so that I have no abandoned my belief in the plan of God at the first sign of difficulty.

It was inevitable that my brothers were terrified of me when we were reunited in Egypt. If I chose to avenge myself on them, they were helpless to escape, and they knew it (Gen 45:3). They had never expected to see me again but I had mused endlessly on the prospect and I'd also seen the guidance of God over the years. I accepted now what I had tried for years to reject: my terrible experiences were not the end of the road, but were often the point at which God opened a new door for the next stage of his plan. He was not playing with me, whatever the cynics might suggest, he was leading a man who had entrusted his life to God.

When Pharaoh put me in power over Egypt, I looked back and saw what I had not seen before: the puzzle was beginning to fit together into a complete picture. I was now in a place it seemed possible that the promise of my dreams could be fulfilled. I had power, my family might come to Egypt, and they would need my authority before they could buy food. All this made me willing to accept the painful experiences which had been part of my difficult journey.

Our reunion might have been achieved with less hardship for me and I had resented much of what happened, but I also began to see how true it was that 'the Lord was with Joseph' (Gen 39:2). I wanted to drum my understanding into my brothers, hoping that if I repeated myself often enough, the message would sink in. I'm not sure that I succeeded, but I tried hard. Four times in as many sentences I told them what I believed, and they listened to me. 'It was to save lives that God sent me ahead of you.' 'But God sent me ahead of you to preserve for you a remnant on earth and to save your lives by a great deliverance.' 'So then, it was not you who sent me here, but God. He made me father to Pharaoh, lord of his entire household and ruler of all Egypt...Now hurry back to my father and say to him, "This is what your son Joseph says: God has made me lord of all Egypt" ' (Gen 45:5, 7–9).

I have already agreed with you that this explanation of my life is still open to question, not least because we're trying to answer questions which cannot yield final answers. We're groping in the dark, but we know that God has given us some light. Did he plan my brothers' assault on me? Does that mean I can't hold them responsible for it? Did he prompt Potiphar's wife, and where does that leave morality? Somehow we have to hold together all sorts of things which appear to be in tension, without justifying physical assault, bitter jealousy, arrogant indulgence, blatant seduction, vicious betrayal, pitiless slavery or unjust punishment. No theory of God's sovereignty is valid which legitimises these deliberate outrages which ruin human life. At the same time, I have to say that although I made some dreadful blunders and suffered deeply, the Lord was with me. He gave me something which others might call 'victory'. That word provokes some people, and it is used at times to describe a selfish triumph which is indifferent to widespread misery. That's now how I'm using the word. I found strength to survive circumstances which otherwise would have crushed me. I came to believe in a purpose for my life which otherwise was futile. I discovered the will to continue and not to give up. I pinned my faith in God, despite the temptation to renounce him for an Egyptian religion which was more immediate and much less demanding. That is what I'm calling 'victory', and I hope you won't object if I ask you to agree with me. After all, it certainly wasn't defeat!

Guidance and the present

I wanted to do the right thing but I didn't always have much choice about what was happening to me. When I had decisions to make, I prayed for God to lead me, trying hard to weigh up all the alternatives before I took any action. I asked him for wisdom as I tried to maintain a scrupulous integrity which was worthy of the God I served. The more I understood his purpose, the more my frustrations calmed and my pain eased, but I was still more than familiar with personal anguish and spiritual rebellion. God's guidance was not a blinding light which helped me to reach total certainty or complete understanding. Other people may claim that, but I know I can't. My progress has been more dogged; I've missed some of the heights but I have clung to God in determined trust. I think I've also avoided some of the pitfalls which have tripped up people who make proud claims for themselves but fall flat on their faces when they hit trouble. Let me share some of the positive ways in which God has guided me that are likely to be relevant for you.

He led me to keep going. I dreamed my dreams, and God planted a seed of faith in me which almost died but never lost its life. In a desert cistern, in the heat of false accusation, in the despair of prison and the awesome responsibility of the famine, I always believed that a different future was coming to me although it was a long time turning up. I had no idea how it could happen and I was often at a complete loss, but I held my faith to myself to avoid ridicule, and I kept going. I believed for the next day, refusing the paralysis which was my only alternative.

He helped me to interpret my circumstances. I lived daily in an awareness of God which convinced no one except me. That was how I made sense of my surroundings. The insinuation that life was all a sinister plot, with me as its chief victim, tempted me again and again, and I felt its full force. I gave my reply and my testimony when I named my sons. I called the first one Manasseh and said, 'It is because God has made me forget all my trouble and all my father's household' (Gen 41:51). If you followed my example you'd have to call your son 'Inner Healing'. The name was as much an act of faith as the celebration of an achievement but the arrival of Manasseh was one of the great moments of my life. I named our second son Ephraim, adding the happy explanation, 'It is because God has made me fruitful in the land of my suffering' (Gen 41:52). I had not hidden from my plight but I had declared a purpose which was far greater than my trials.

He challenged me to forgive. My strong belief about the purpose of my life led me to forgive my brothers. The will of God had become more important to me than my own feelings and I knew I had to release them from the bitterness I had felt for years. I did not excuse them, I forgave them. God was not condoning their treachery, He was destroying its power to be the final word in our relationship. I know how carefully you must tread when you talk like this because some people are quick to accuse you of justifying evil or of creating a God without morality. But surely you can see I'm not saying anything like that. I am sharing the story of my life in which the wrongs we inflict on each other have not been able to thwart what God has wanted to do. Every time I feared the final curtain had come down, he moved me on to the next act.

He gave me peace. Whenever I wanted God to speak to me, he seemed to call me to a definite acceptance of his will. In the Egyptian prison I tried to manipulate a freedom which would remove me from that will—I asked the cup-bearer to put in such a good word for me with Pharaoh that I'd be set free (Gen 40:14, 23). You can't blame me for trying to get out of prison, but I was scheming for something which God was not giving me. My freedom would take me a long way from Pharaoh and just as far from the will of God. He gave me peace about the whole thing, and I stayed in prison until he led me out. If God wants to bring you to power, he'll prepare you first, and the training can be tough. I waited a further two years, until Pharaoh obliged me with his dream of the Nile with seven sleek and seven ugly cows, which he followed up with a similar dream of healthy and scorched ears of corn (Gen 41:1–7).

Guidance and the future

The fact of God's guidance gave me courage for a future which appeared bleak to me, but he led me to move ahead, despite my uncertainty about what might be hiding round the corner. He kept me trusting a purpose which was still far from complete.

Let's go back to the point where I'd met my brothers in Egypt but had not yet announced myself to them. They thought they were pleading with a stranger who held absolute authority over them. He had accused them of being spies from Canaan, and they were too afraid to be indignant. In my mock anger, I demanded that they fetch Benjamin to Egypt (Gen 42:14–16). What a shock to them if I had told them to fetch 'our' youngest brother! I must admit, the thought did cross my mind. But I restrained my humour, and told them that I feared God (Gen 42:18). The 'fear of God' is an important part of our necessary response to him, and it has always mattered a lot to me. But what do I mean by 'the fear of God'? I think it holds together a strong trust and yet a humble caution. It describes an awareness of God which draws confidence but compels respect. You can't come too near him, but you don't have to cringe far away. Our God is a majestic God, and we have to approach him on his terms, not ours. There is an irresistible attraction about him which has become a vital part of our Hebrew worship. My obedience and my grateful recognition of his guidance spring directly from my 'fear' of him. It doesn't force me to retreat but welcomes me into a relationship which adds friendship to my worship. In a nutshell 'the fear of God' is a way of describing a right response to him which has a radical effect on our daily life. When I told my brothers that I feared God, I was assuring them that I would prove true and not false in my dealings with them; they could trust a man who feared God. So far as I know none of our local religions have any corresponding concept of God.

My dreams, of course, were an integral part of the way God led me into the future. Far from indulging the arrogance of a teenager, they prepared me for a series of ordeals which tested me to the limit but also helped me to be willing to serve him. When I met my brothers in Egypt, I saw how God had kept his original promise to me (Gen 42:8–9).

All this has reminded me of my great grandfather Abraham. God gave him a promise which took years to fulfil: 'A son coming from your own body will be your heir' (Gen 15:4). Abraham kept his faith in that promise until the day my grandfather Isaac was born. Now I agree with you that this is an extreme, almost ridiculous example because it was all so unlikely. But God's word offered Abraham and Sarah peace of mind through long years of waiting, and it prevented the awful shock they would have suffered if Sarah became pregnant at her age with no previous warning! Each time I grew impatient as a child, some adult sat me down to regale me with the shining example of patience shown by my illustrious ancestors. I thought little boys were supposed to be kept in ignorance of the facts of life, but it suited most adults to forget that when they lectured me. Adults will tell a child anything if peace and quiet are at stake, and that's one of the first lessons the child learns when he begins to knock his parents into the required shape. Abraham's experience of God did for him what my dreams did for me, and we both waited for a future which took years to materialise, often seeming to become more remote as time passed.

I viewed the sons of my grandson Makir as tokens of this assured future, and I was thrilled to bless them when he placed them on my knees (Gen 50:23). All the family stood around, nervous and ready to jump if the old man dropped the babies. I pretended not to notice because their apprehension irritated me; I've held more babies than they've had hot dinners. They were treasured moments when I was allowed to nurse these tiny signs of the future, and I saw God's purpose stretching way beyond my own life.

I doubt if I have more than a few days left and then I shall die. A foreboding about the treatment of my people after my death is plaguing me at the moment. A new Pharaoh will not feel himself bound to continue the protection I have enjoyed, and I'm well aware how much popularity I lost when I took tough measures to eke out our dwindling stocks towards the end of the famine years (Gen 47:13). In some areas people coped well, but there was terrible suffering for those who had few resources to buy food and no means of transport to the storage depots. As I exchanged food for livestock, and then food for land, the nation vented its resentment on me (Gen 47:20–21). We had to take even harsher measures, and I exchanged seed for a share in the harvest, a form of taxation far more serious than anyone had ever known in Egypt, although we knew of such deprivations in other countries. I issued an edict that a fifth of all produce would belong to Pharaoh (Gen 47:26). Those who had been just grateful to survive grew to resent their poverty, focusing their grudges on the man they felt had initiated the problem. I am worried that the bitterness which can no longer reach me will reach my people who have an uncanny knack for survival and prosperity, which infuriates less resilient nations. This is already well noted. 'The Israelites settled in Egypt in the region of Goshen. They acquired property there and were fruitful and increased greatly in number' (Gen 47:27).

Maybe I was foolish, maybe I did the right thing, but I'm anxious for these babies on my knees. I cannot guarantee them the comfortable future which I covet for them. But God will keep his word; only its timing is hidden from us. I have made things clear to my brothers and I think they have heard me well: 'I am about to die. But God will surely come to your aid and take you up out of this land to the land he promised on oath to Abraham, Isaac and Jacob' (Gen 50:24).

Postscript

Joseph desperately wanted to finish this book. He did so only days before he died, and his dying wishes were not ignored—'God will surely come to your aid, and then you must carry my bones up from this place' (Gen 50:25)—an indication of the tremendous honour in which his people held him. They made every effort to fulfil the dying wishes of their great Patriarch.

'So Joseph died at the age of a hundred and ten. And after they embalmed him he was placed in a coffin in Egypt' (Gen 50:26). Even then, Joseph was not consigned to distant memory. When the children of Israel left Egypt, Joseph's remains went with them, a fitting tribute to a great man. 'Moses took the bones of Joseph with him because Joseph had made the sons of Israel swear an oath. He had said, "God will surely come to your aid, and then you must carry my bones up with you from this place" ' (Ex 13:19–20).

[illegible]

[illegible] the [illegible] with [illegible]

[illegible]

I Am Jeremiah

by Alan Pain

Meet Jeremiah—the prophet who never wanted to be a prophet. Visionary of rotten figs, smasher of clay pots, and gate-crasher of His Majesty's banquet—wearing nothing but a cloak and a yoke.

From the stock to the docks, and the cell to the well, he was, as the saying goes, a 'right Jeremiah'.

Or was he?

This book penetrates beyond the doom and gloom to the heart of Jeremiah's message—a stark and heartbreaking one, yet carrying the promise of new hope. A message for our times.

'In a movingly personal yet humorous account, written as if by Jeremiah himself, Alan Pain paints a vivid but accurate word picture of one of the Old Testament's most colourful prophets. When you've read the book you'll want to read the Book.'

—**Derek Copley**
Principal, Moorlands Bible College

ALAN PAIN is Minister of Sutton Coldfield Baptist Church, a few miles outside Birmingham.

Kingsway Publications